ne année.   Prix : Cinq cent   Jeudi 28 Juillet 1892.

LA GAUDRIOLE

Journal de Joyeux Récits, Contes ... *illustrés*

PARAISSANT DEU...

ABONNEMENTS

PARIS ET PROVINCE

UN AN........ 7 FR.
SIX-MOIS .... 4 »
TROIS MOIS.. 3 »
Étranger, port en plus.

5, Rue Geoffroy-Marie
PARIS

...tivement peur; ... l'ait détachée de moi. Grand Dieu !
...s son boudoir, je ... ...mande quel charme elle peut trouver
...lique cela. ... ...xistence intolérable.
— Je l'explique par ... ...ne connais pas mieux les femmes?
... tu n'étais pas ... ...ouve cette volupté raffinée, exquise,
... tu as aimé comme ... ...rembler, ramper devant elle un homme
...ore, peut-être, la ... ...pieds six pouces, ayant bravé la mort
...abanère se leva ... ...is, très beau, — soit dit sans le flatter,
... les épaules de so... ...i pourrait, toute superbe qu'elle est,
— Je vais te dire ... ...ar terre d'une chiquenaude. Une seule
...nière, au momen... ...étonne.

For Deirdre,
Best Regards,
Winston Conrad

Hemingway's France

Hemingway's France

Images of the Lost Generation

by Winston Conrad

Design by Tom Morgan

WOODFORD PRESS

For Paulette

Book and cover design: Tom Morgan, Blue Design, www.bluedes.com

Library of Congress Catalog Card Number: 00-103563
ISBN: 0-942627-62-8

Distributed by Andrews McMeel Publishing, Kansas City, MO.

Woodford Press
5900 Hollis Street, Suite K
Emeryville, CA 94608
www.woodfordpub.com

Daniel C. Ross, CEO and Publisher
C. David Burgin, Editor and Publisher
William F. Duane, Senior Vice President

Associate publishers:
Franklin M. Dumm
William W. Scott, Esq.
William B. McGuire, Esq.
Gary Notti, CPA

Pages 2-3: A streetcar on its way up Rue Soufflot to the Panthéon. This street scene is typical of those in Paris in the 1920s. (RV)

Pages 4: Gerald Murphy's backdrop for "Within the Quota," presented by the Swedish Ballet at the Théâtré des Champs-Elysees, Paris, 1923. The program featured music by Cole Porter. (EHMD)

This page: The cabaret club Moulin-Rouge, photographed by Atget, shortly before Hemingway's arrival in Paris. It still draws a crowd to its shows. (PC)

Pages 8-9: At the Hôtel de la Mère Poularde on Mont-Saint-Michel in 1944 (left to right): Time correspondent Bill Walton, Madame Chevalier, Ernest Hemingway, an Army Signal Corps photographer, Maurice Chevalier, and Life photographer Bob Capa. (JFKL)

Page 10: Les Folies-Bergère star Josephine Baker performing her "Banana Dance." (RV)

Page 13: A portrait of Ernest Hemingway taken in 1923, which hung in Sylvia Beach's bookstore Shakespeare and Company. (PUL)

CONTENTS

PARIS

CHAMPERRET

LA CHAPELLE

MONTMARTRE

Montmartre Cimetery

Sacre Coeur

MONCEAU

PARK de MONCEAU

Russian Church

Hopital Lariboisière

North Ry. Sta.

Santé

St. Vincent de Paul

Strasburg Ry. Station Hospital Militaire

Prison St. Lazare

Hospice St. Louis

Trinité Ch.

St. Lazare & Western Ry. Sta.

Arc de Triomphe

American Church

Hippodrome

Opera Grand Hotel

Madeleine

Pal. de l'Elysée

English Embassy

Ministry of Justice

Palais des Beaux Arts

Chamber of Commerce

PLACE DES VICTOIRES

PLACE VENDOME

PLACE DE LA CONCORDE

Jardin des Tuileries

Théatre Français

Bourse

St. Eustache

Bourse de Commerce

Conservatory

PLACE DE LA REPUBLIQUE

Palais Royal

Palais du Louvre

National Printing office

Palais du Trocadéro

Manuf. des Tabacs

D'Orsay

Palais Bourbon

Station D'ORSAY

Quai du Louvre

Pl. du Carrousel

The Arts

Institute

Mint

ILE DE LA CITE

Hotel de Ville

Barracks

PLACE DES VOSGES

EXPOSITION

Hotel des Invalides

Hopital de la Charité

Palais de Justice

Hotel Dieu

Notre Dame

ILE ST. LOUIS

Morgue

Ecole Militaire

Hopital Laennec

St. Sulpice

Palais du Sénat

Collège de France

Jardin du Luxembourg

Panthéon

Jardin des Plantes

Prison

St. J. Baptiste

Gas Works

Lycée Buffon

Western Ry. Sta.

Lycée Montaigne

Lyons Ry. Sta.

Hopital St. Jacques

Pasteur Inst.

Mont Parnasse Cemetery

Hopital du Val de Grace

Hopital Ricord

Observatory

Hopital de la Salpetriere

SEINE

My Moveable Feast

W. H. Auden once observed that "no two people ever read the same book." Likewise, one might declare that no two people ever live in the same Paris, that each of its visitors leaves with unique, indelible impressions of the city.

But visitors to Paris and the rest of France also come away with shared feelings. After making eight trips to Europe I understood why Ernest Hemingway cherished France in general and its capital in particular.

Once I sampled French food, culture and traditions, I found myself comparing them — almost always favorably — to their counterparts back home. When it came time to return to the United States from one of my trips to Europe, I'd dwell somewhat sadly on protagonist Jake Barnes's comment in Hemingway's first novel, *The Sun Also Rises*: "I hated to leave France. Life was so simple in France."

Although my time in France didn't yield anything quite like the experiences Hemingway had among his "lost generation" contemporaries and as a World War II correspondent and self-styled commando, I was lucky enough to see the country from disparate perspectives. On more than one of my eight trips I hitchhiked around, or simply walked. On another I stayed in Paris with my great aunt and her husband, the Vicomte de Bonchamps, in their lavish Avenue Foch apartment. On later visits, I strolled through the Luxembourg Gardens, pushing my young sons around in a stroller. On still other visits, I mixed conventional tourism with a lot of photography and research.

As I looked back on them, my journeys seemed to affirm everything about France that Hemingway celebrated in his writing, whether we were drinking Cahors wine, baking in the Provençal sun, betting on horses at the track, viewing masterpieces in museums, or simply gazing at tiled Parisian rooftops from a garret in the 7th arrondissement.

This book is my attempt to illustrate Hemingway's attachment to France and its City of Light, to connect us with the magic and romance that inspired him to write wonderful stories and great books.   —W.S.C.

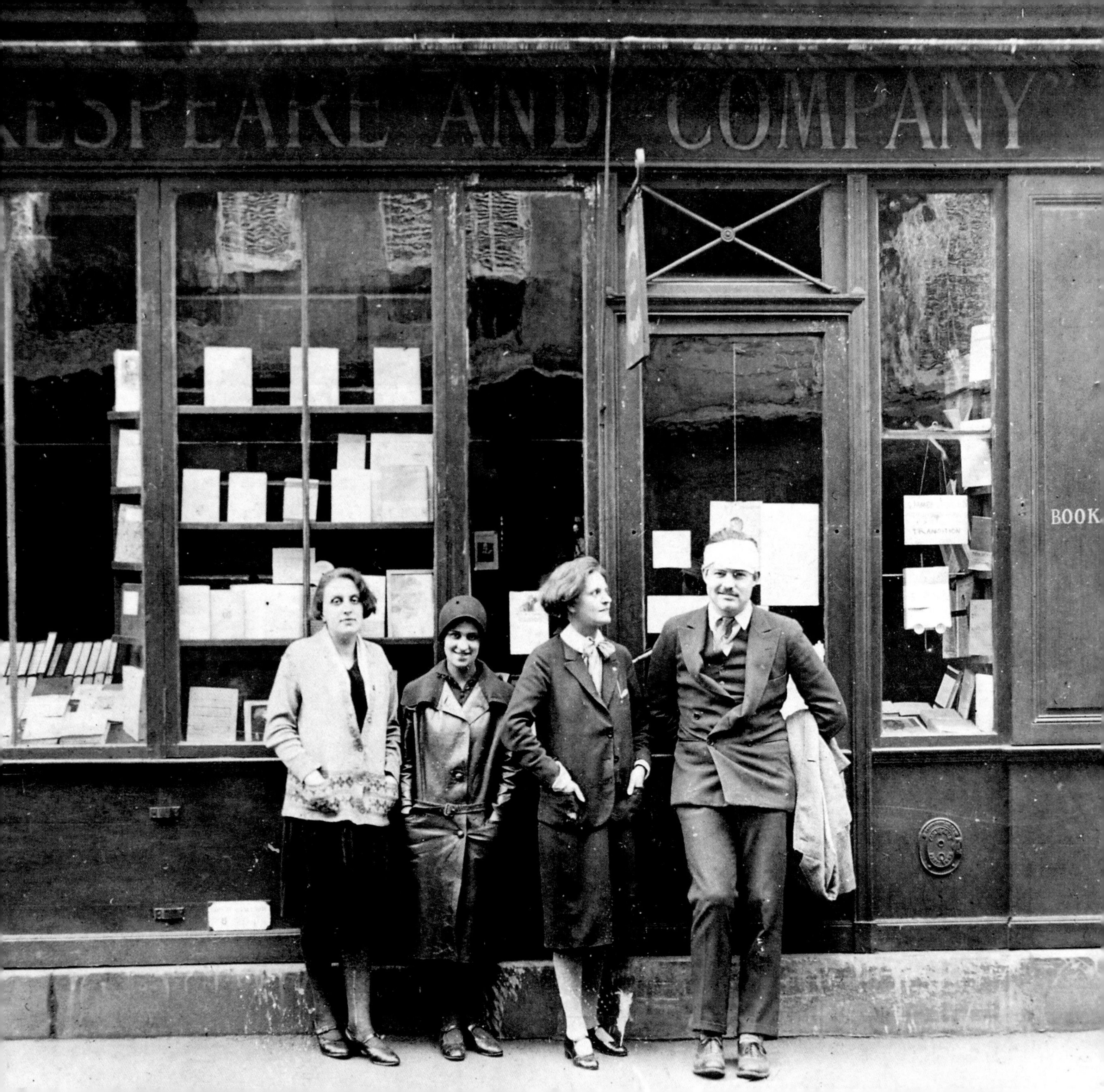
ESPEARE AND COMPANY
BOOK

Chapter One

The Literary Scene in Paris

"Paris in the 1920s" still evokes wonder as one of the most flamboyant and creative periods in modern Western cultural history. Pablo Picasso, Georges Braque, James Joyce, T. S. Eliot, Gertrude Stein, F. Scott Fitzgerald, Ezra Pound, Gerald and Sara Murphy, Cole Porter, Sergey Diaghilev, and scores of other artists, musicians and writers came to the Left Bank of the Seine to form a dazzling vortex of talent and experimentation. From their studios and garrets emerged the new styles of art and literature known collectively as modernism.

After World War I, many of America's most serious artists decided that France was the place

Opposite: Sylvia Beach, third from left, and Ernest Hemingway outside Beach's Shakespeare and Company bookstore, a primary resource for Hemingway and his colleagues. Myrsine Moschos, a longtime clerk in the shop, stands at the far left, next to her sister Helene, who ran errands for Beach. (PUL) Above: Gertrude Stein, with her godson, Jack "Bumby" Hemingway. (JFKL)

Hemingway with his second wife, the chic Pauline Pfeiffer, an assistant to the Paris editor of Vogue *magazine. Four years older than Hemingway, Pauline had insinuated herself into the Hemingway household while he was still married to his first wife, Hadley. Pauline and Hemingway were married in Paris in May 1927. (JFKL)*

Opposite: Hemingway with his first son, John Hadley Nicanor Hemingway, nicknamed "Bumby." Hemingway's first wife, Hadley, gave birth to the child on October 10, 1923, in Toronto, where Hemingway worked as a reporter for the Toronto Daily Star. *(JFKL)*

munity of writers, poets, and literary-magazine publishers — represented the future of literature. Hemingway celebrated its spirit decades later in *A Moveable Feast*, his sentimental recollection of his literary coming-of-age in the City of Light. "If you are lucky enough to have lived in Paris as a young man," he wrote several years before his death in 1961, "then wherever you go for the rest of your life, it stays with you, for Paris is a moveable feast."

When Anderson, a successful and seasoned writer, told Hemingway, a native of Oak Park, Illinois, that Paris was where he might find his voice, Hemingway listened.

Anderson gave Hemingway letters of introduction to the bookseller Sylvia Beach, the avant-garde fiction stylist Gertrude Stein, the Irish literary colossus James Joyce, and the brilliant, generous-to-a-fault Ezra Pound. On the Monday after Thanksgiving, 1921, the twenty-two-year-old Hemingway and his new bride, Hadley Richardson, sailed for Paris aboard the French Line's *Léopoldina*. "The world is a jail," exclaimed Hadley, "and we're going to break it together." A few days before Christmas the handsome couple checked into the Jacob et d' Angleterre (now the Hotel d' Angleterre, on the Rue Jacob), which was full of interesting, ec-

to be. Ernest Hemingway entered this world determined to write what he saw. His was the voice of youth disillusioned by an awful war and seeking life in friendship, love and the purifying effects of nature. In Paris, Hemingway became Hemingway, and in the process created a prose style that, for many writers, is still a benchmark in American literature.

The writer Sherwood Anderson, himself disillusioned with American social strictures, instilled in Hemingway the notion that Paris — in particular the expatriate American com-

Left Bank bookshops have long been excellent sources for the literary-minded. "I really thought one could work far better there than anywhere on Earth," American novelist Thomas Wolfe once said of Paris. (WSC)

The tale was full of lost-generation archetypes based in most cases on members of Hemingway's circle, who went to the bullfights with a plethora of emotional baggage. Stein first heard the term used in inauspicious circumstances, in an automobile garage where her Model T was undergoing repairs by a young mechanic who had served in the Great War. In Stein's presence, his employer reprimanded the callow veteran for his alleged ineptitude, and dismissed him as yet another distracted, unfocused and unreliable member of *la génération perdue*. Impressed by the remark, Stein later applied it to Hemingway and his disillusioned contemporaries, telling Hemingway that they were a lost generation whose members drank themselves to death and wasted their lives.

Stein's observation echoed in Hemingway's mind — it was exactly in keeping with his conviction that the war had prematurely stripped his generation of youth's illusions and cast it adrift. He appropriated his mentor's remark for the working title of his first serious novel, but *The Lost Generation* (née *Fiesta*) eventually became *The Sun Also Rises*, which enshrines Stein's words in one of its epigraphs. The *Sun* shone warmly on Hemingway, and his literary career bloomed. Success cemented his relationship with Charles Scribner's Sons, which went on to publish the author's books for the rest of his life.

In the retelling, the story of Hemingway's literary emergence sounds fairly simple. But in fact his transformation into the foremost writer of his era was as convoluted for him as artistic transformations were for many of his colleagues. They all were trying to find their way in a very complicated and civilized country — a country that had won their hearts but was not their own.

Two sphinx statues overlooking the courtyard to Hemingway's third Parisian apartment at the fashionable address of 6 Rue Férou, near the Luxembourg Gardens. (WSC)

Chapter Two

Paris Yesterday and Today

"There is a magic in the name France ... It is a very old magic. France is a broad and lovely country. The loveliest country that I know. It is impossible to write impartially about a country when you love it."

ERNEST HEMINGWAY
"THE FRANCO-GERMAN SITUATION"
TORONTO DAILY STAR 1923

In the latter part of the nineteenth century it was fashionable for wealthy Americans to make extended visits to Paris. They brought with them customs foreign to Gallic ways. Some French were alarmed by *nouvelles* Yankee notions like feminism, fearing assertive American women might similarly "Americanize" their females. The influx of American

Opposite: The River Seine. "You expected to be sad in the Fall," Hemingway wrote in A Moveable Feast. *"Part of you died each year when the leaves fell from the trees and their branches were bare against the wind and the cold, wintry light. But you knew there would always be spring, as you knew the river would flow again after it was frozen." (Photo by Atget; WSC) Above: The arches of the Eiffel Tower. (WSC)*

A gargoyle overlooking Paris from the top of Notre-Dame cathedral. (WSC)

Along with the vogue in American inventions — among them the lightbulb, the telegraph, and typewriters — came wealthy American tourists who traveled to Europe seeking "culture." They found it waiting and available, at extraordinarily low prices, in Paris.

There was nothing in America comparable to strolling along the river Seine or on Baron Karl Hausmann's newly built grand boulevards, which linked the *quartiers*, each like a separate town within the city. (Some of these boulevards, such as Saint-Germain and Saint-Michel, which connected the old Latin Quarter with the rest of the city, would not be completed until after World War I ended.) Construction of the boulevards encouraged the proliferation of cafés and, in turn, attracted the artists. The bohemian culture thrived.

For Americans, the lopsided dollar/franc exchange rate turned Paris into a ready-made bohemia of cheap everything — artist's lofts, hotel rooms, and hundreds of intimate cafés for watching life go by on summer evenings. The boulevards, wrote Henry James, were "a long chain of cafés, each one with its little promontory of chairs and tables projecting into the sea of asphalt. These promontories are doubtless not exactly islands of the blessed, peopled though

money, however, was seductive. The American tendency toward things big challenged the French sense of scale. (Upon its completion in 1889, the Eiffel Tower was deemed *très Américain.*) Traffic jams were regarded as a transplanted American phenomenon. As the new century got underway, more Americans strode confidently down the gangways of steamships, puffing big Havana cigars, demanding ice in their drinks and other odd comforts such as full-immersion baths and telephones that actually worked.

Hemingway first glimpsed Paris on his way to the Italian front during World War I. (JFKL)

some of them may be with sirens addicted to beer, but they may help you pass a hot evening."

Even middle-class Americans could afford grand hotels like Cesar Ritz's luxurious namesake, opened in 1898 to offer "all the refinements that a prince could ask for in his own home." The performing arts flourished and attracted top-ranked stars of the day. Every week, half a million Parisians went to the theater.

After World War I, the Age of Travel gave way to the Age of Tourism, and Americans arrived en masse. A good many of these arrivistes had visited Paris as American doughboys, experienced some of the exotic pleasures of Continental life, and then gone home to a straitlaced America of the Prohibition era.

Ernest Hemingway was among the many returned ex-soldiers for whom American life no longer held much allure. He had been fascinated with Paris from his first glimpse of it, when he was eighteen, during a brief stopover on his way to the Italian front. By comparison, his hometown of Oak Park, Illinois, a comfortable suburb of Chicago, seemed stifling. When his family's Victrola record player played the scratchy lyrics of a popular song that asked "How are you gonna keep 'em down on the farm once they've seen Paree?" Hemingway

The street view from the kitchen window of Hemingway's apartment on the Rue Cardinal Lemoine. (JFKL)

39

knew exactly what they'd seen, and he determined to see it again.

As the 1920s commenced, American intellectuals chafed under the perceived provincialism of the time. For the country's writers, poets, social critics and artists, the fabled laissez-faire attitudes of France beckoned like an Eden of creativity, a place to where a confused generation might retreat and find a center. As English poet Malcolm Cowley wrote in his book *Exile's Return*, "it seemed time for a great migration eastward into the new prairies of the mind."

Never before had there been such a large migration of artists and writers from America to a foreign land, in particular to an ancient city steeped in such an inviting mix of lore, custom and liberty. Glowing accounts of the city's phenomenal beauty and the sensuousness of French culture turned attention to Paris, even if some of its perceived pleasures and promise proved to be products of wishful thinking.

"Paris was a very old city," a reflective Hemingway noted much later, "and we were young and nothing was simple there ..." But for

Gilded in golf leaf, this statue overlooks Pont Alexandre III. (WSC)

an extraordinary few, the City of Light was a portal into a world of legendary achievement.

In the chic and exotic sidewalk soirées of the Left Bank's bistros and cafés, the intellectuals, the artists and their followers created the public image of the lost generation — which, in spite of its supposed spiritual poverty, looked to most like it was having an awfully good time. Paris, said Hemingway (mimicking the extravagant speech of the wealthy English drifters who decorated the scene), was "simply grand." It was made even grander on the Hemingways' arrival by the prospect of exchanging each of their American dollars for twenty-five French francs. By 1926, the franc's value against the dollar had fallen by half and a dollar bought fifty francs, enabling an American to enjoy a three-course *haute cuisine* meal for the equivalent of twenty cents. Never had the notion of being a poor artist been so appealing, at least to those with American passports.

The twenties was a giddy time of booming stock markets and American confidence and excess that F. Scott Fitzgerald dubbed the Jazz Age. Yet Paris loomed in the minds of many as a rival to New York in its role as America's literary (if not publishing) capital.

The financial balloon that floated many expatriates above the requirements of a workaday life popped in 1929 when Wall Street crashed. In Paris the lost generation became the financially lost generation.

Some expatriates returned home only to find themselves feeling out of place in Depression-era America. Many of the American self-exiles, however, managed to stay on. A new, more international group formed that included many Londoners, Italians, and German Jews. Despite hard times, a trickle of bold

Americans kept arriving. One, a passionate and earthy man from Brooklyn named Henry Miller, followed in Hemingway's footsteps and later assumed the mantle of the quintessential avant-garde American writer in Paris.

Paris, Hemingway remarked, was still the city "best organized for a writer to write in that there is." At sidewalk cafés under chestnut trees in blossom, writers could pencil words for hours on end for the price of a cup of coffee. Their privacy was virtually guaranteed. "If you are a writer," observed Gertrude Stein, "you have privileges, if you are a painter you have privileges, and it is pleasant." The thirties and forties changed much of Paris, along with most of the rest of the world. Yet — improbably but happily — many of the pleasant places where Hemingway, Stein, Miller and other artists and writers took their privilege have survived.

The fountains in the Place de L'Observatoire look much the same today as when Hemingway strolled by them. (JFKL)

The River Seine

The river was dark and a bateau mouche went by, all bright with lights, going fast and quiet up and out of sight under the bridge. Down the river was Notre Dame squatting against the night sky. We crossed to the left bank of the Seine by the wooden foot-bridge from the Quai de Bethune, and stopped on the bridge and looked down the river ...

THE SUN ALSO RISES

Without La Seine, Paris would not be Paris. The river fascinated Hemingway, who during boyhood fishing adventures in Michigan had acquired a near-mystical fascination with rivers.

Hemingway liked to stroll along the Seine to clear his mind. He browsed the old bookstalls along the *quais*, and occasionally found recently published books in English at good prices. In his memoir *A Moveable Feast* he recalled his routine of buying sausage, a loaf of bread and wine and then sitting at the river's edge to read the books and observe the fishermen. "I would walk along the quais when I had finished work or when I was trying to think something out. It was easier to think if I was walking and doing something or seeing people doing something that they understood."

Hemingway liked to talk to the fishermen about technique, sometimes in the company of his firstborn son, Bumby — John Hadley Nicanor Hemingway, also known as Jack. (Jack would eventually surpass his father as an expert fly fisherman.) On the banks of the Seine Ernest and Bumby sometimes watched the workmen fishing. "The good spots to fish changed with the height of the river," Ernest later recounted, "and the fisherman used long, jointed cane poles but fished with very fine leaders and light gear and quill floats and expertly baited the piece of water that they fished."

Afterwards, father and son would sometimes dine on the fresh catch at La Pêche Miraculeuse, an open-air restaurant built over the river. Hemingway called it "a place out of a Maupassant story with the view over the river as Sisley had painted it."

Hemingway was not the only writer fascinated by the river. James Joyce insisted on residing near the Seine when he visited Paris, and cherished his daily strolls along the river. This strict ritual, he said, rejuvenated his soul. Hemingway understood the great Irishman's affection for the swift-flowing water. "With the fishermen and the life on the river," he wrote in *A Moveable Feast*, "the beautiful barges with their life on board, the tugs with their smokestacks that folded back to pass under the bridges, pulling a tow of barges, the great elms on the stone banks of the river, the plane trees and in some places the poplars, I could never be lonely along the river."

Though the Seine is perhaps best known as the stream dividing Paris, its passage through the City of Light is but a small portion of its journey across France to the English Channel. Likewise, Hemingway's five fabled expatriate years in France tend to dominate our attention, even though he lived for twelve years in Key West, Florida, and for almost two decades in Cuba. The point is not that he spent a relatively short time in Paris but that he accomplished so much there. In those sixty-odd months, he transformed himself from an unknown and callow Midwesterner into a sophisticated citizen of the world.

Hemingway's literary odyssey was unlike that of any other in American writing, a journey that commenced in a humble room overlooking the rooftops of a poor neighborhood in Paris. Some years later he described his love of Paris in the short story "The Snows of Kilimanjaro," transforming it into nostalgic musing by one of his reflective characters, Harry: "There never was another part of Paris that he loved like that, the sprawling trees, the old white plastered houses painted brown below, the long green of the autobus in that round square, the purple flower dye upon the paving, the sudden drop down the hill of the rue Cardinal Lemoine to the River ..."

Opposite: Le Pont Neuf. Hemingway, like James Joyce, liked to stroll along the Seine. (WSC)

Chapter Three

Cafés, Restaurants and Nightlife

"I could always go to a café to write and could work all morning over a café crème while the waiters cleaned and swept out the café and it gradually grew warmer."

EARNEST HEMINGWAY
A MOVEABLE FEAST

The open-air cafés of Paris offered refuge from the machinations of the city. They were sanctuaries for socializing or simply savoring the beauties of life over a refreshment. In the 1920s, no city in the world had so many attractive cafés, remarkable restaurants and exhilarating cabarets. Some Paris nightclubs

Opposite: Le Sélect, in Montparnasse, a popular meeting place for local and American-expatriate writers, artists and sports lovers. (JFKL) Above: F. Scott Fitzgerald was the foremost chronicler of the Jazz Age. This 1922 dust jacket was illustrated by John Held, Jr., the most popular cartoonist of the flapper era. (PUL)

Statues of Chinese dignitaries (magots) still adorn the Café des Deux-Magots, on Boulevard St-Germain. (WSC)

featured a sensational new art form, *le jazz hot*, imported from America, which added to the mystique of the city known for liberated and often naughty nightlife, a place where, as Cole Porter put it, anything goes.

The café serves as a meeting place and the perfect spot for the sport of people watching, which in France is a national pastime. Anaïs Nin summed up the value of the café by noting that "The hours I have spent in cafés are the only ones I call living, apart from writing." (It was a curious statement for a woman who wrote in Paris about sensual sexual liaisons, for which she reputedly had a considerable appetite.)

In his 5th arrondissement neighborhood, Hemingway would visit Café de la Contrescarpe, La Chope, Au Nègre Joyeux and Café des Arts. He avoided the excessively seedy haunts. He also walked to the Latin Quarter, where at the Café de Flore and Café des Deux-Magots, on Boulevard St-Germain, he would meet up with his ever-expanding circle of artistic acquaintances. In his memoir *Paris Was Our Mistress*, Samuel Putnam wrote that "the Café des Deux-Magots itself was something like neutral ground, a vague No Man's Land between opposing camps and between the Right Bank and the Left, being a favorite resort of journalists and of Sorbonne professors invading another Bohemia than the one to which they were accustomed in the vicinity of the Boul Mich."

The name Deux-Magots derives from the fact that there was once a shop at the same location that dealt in Asian merchandise. Inside, patrons sat at quiet tables under large old mirrors and two porcelain figures — Chinese dignitaries (the magots) — mounted on center posts.

Across the Boulevard St-Germain squats Brasserié Lipp, where Ernest and Hadley went for sausage with potatoes cooked in olive oil,

Hemingway often visited Brasserié Lipp, which in later years attracted high-profile customers such as French President François Mitterrand. *"It was a quick walk to Lipp's,"* Hemingway wrote in A Moveable Feast, *"and every place I passed that my stomach noticed as quickly as my eyes or my nose made the walk an added pleasure."* The Dingo Bar (inset), a favorite of American expatriates in the 1920s, is now called the Auberge de Venise. (WSC)

51

and for a *demi* or *distingué* of draft beer. Just down the street is Le Pré aux Clercs, the first restaurant the Hemingways frequented after they arrived in Paris, in late 1921.

Around the corner is Brasserié l'Escorialles, known in the 1920s as the Café Michaud, the scene of a poignant if amusing episode recounted by Hemingway in *A Moveable Feast*. Scott Fitzgerald, doubting his sexual adequacy — his wife, Zelda, had told him he did not measure up and could not possibly satisfy any woman — submitted at Hemingway's request to a brief inspection of his private parts in the café's restroom. (Hemingway declared them quite adequate, and encouraged Scott to observe the male statues in the Louvre — proof positive that Zelda's slur was as misguided as it was mean-spirited.)

Work was paramount for Hemingway, who used the café both as studio and office. His favorite public writing place was the Closerie des Lilas, at the end of Boulevard Montparnasse, a few long blocks from the Boulevard Raspail, which was the center of café society. After walking down the hill from his apartment near the Place de la Contrescarpe, passing the mammoth columns of the Panthéon, Hemingway would settle down to write. At La Closerie des Lilas, which was not much visited by the idle members of Paris's expatriate society, he would find warmth and encouragement in a café crème and, if undisturbed, he would complete his daily quota of words. At the end of each day's writing, Hemingway would tally up his word count and enter the total into a ledger.

After work, Hemingway often met up with the other writers and artists in smaller, more intimate places like the Dingo Bar, on the Rue Delambre, now known as L'Auberge de Venise.

The water closet at Brasserié l'Escorialles, formerly Michaud, where Hemingway conducted the famous "inspection" of F. Scott Fitzgerald. (WSC)
Opposite: Touting the name of nineteenth century French poet Paul Verlaine, this restaurant on the rue Descartes anchors the building where Hemingway wrote his first stories. "Up in that room," he wrote in A Moveable Feast, *"I decided that I would write one story about each thing that I knew about. (WSC)*

Café des Arts — around the corner from Hemingway's first apartment, off Place de la Contrescarpe — continues the outdoor café tradition. (WSC)

Hemingway's Paris. "I had never been in a madhouse before I went to Montparnasse," Charters recounted. "I had never seen people drink to get drunk; never seen artists, writers, nobles, American sailors, and doubtful women mingle on equal terms without reserve."

In his introduction to Charters's memoir, Hemingway wrote that "if his book has only one-half of his charm, one-quarter of his knowledge, and one-quarter of his experience it should still be a fairly intoxicating volume. I wish it were not about Montparnasse because that is a dismal place. But Jimmy could make it very cheerful when he was behind the bar."

A master mixologist, Charters claimed in his book to have concocted a powerful aphrodisiac cocktail he called the Jimmy Special. "I must tell you of a cocktail I invented while I was at the Dingo that had a powerful effect on some of the Quarterites ... two stiff drinks of it will have some surprising effects!" he claimed. "On women this drink had the effect of causing them to undress in public, and it often kept me busy wrapping overcoats around nude ladies! But even knowing this did not prevent some of the feminine contingent from asking for the Jimmy Special. I wish I had a hundred francs

In the 1920s the Dingo was run by Jimmy "the Barman" Charters, whose storytelling attracted a faithful clientele who eventually followed him over to Le Falstaff. Charters was a savvy and voluble character with whom Hemingway often discussed horse racing and boxing. Hemingway wrote the introduction to Charters's memoir *This Must Be the Place*, a work ghostwritten by Morrill Cody. The barman's tales of the odd characters who spiced the population of Montparnasse in the Jazz Age were later published under the title

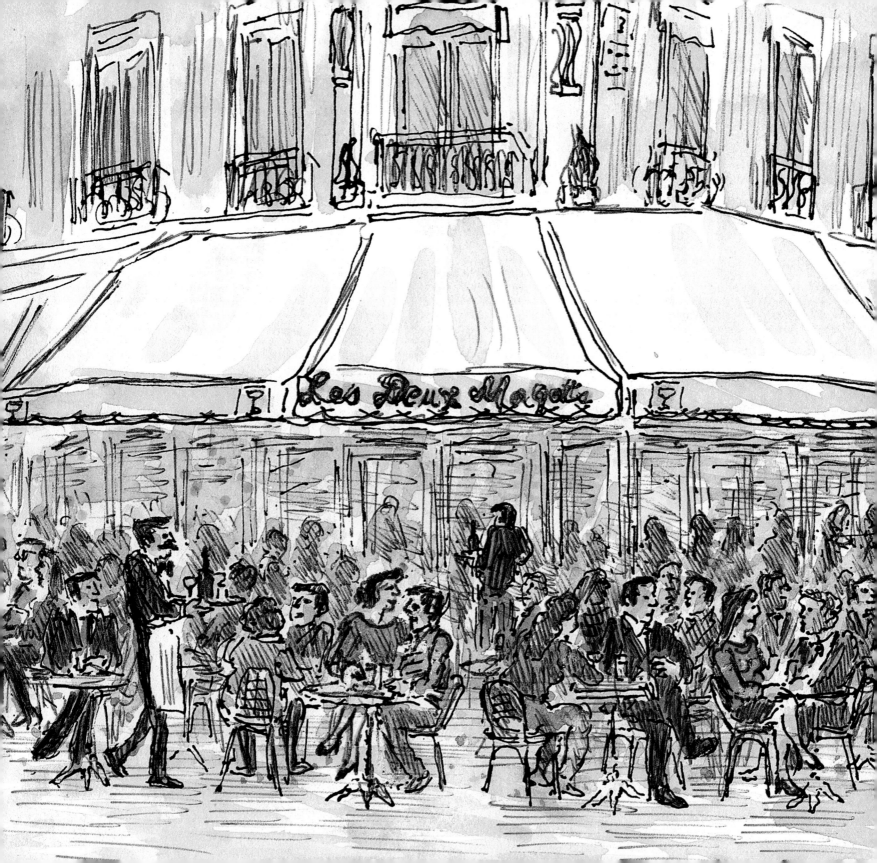

Café de Flore on a cold winter day. (WSC)

pagne and we almost always began with caviar. Our guests were invited to take baths ... Some evenings were rather Pompeiian. The bath could hold four."

When Hemingway heard that Harry and a young woman had committed suicide in a New York hotel room, he wrote to Scott Fitzgerald of his sadness over the loss. Ezra Pound poetically declared that "Crosby's life was a religious manifestation. His death was ... death from excessive vitality. A vote of confidence in the Cosmos." Suicide wove its way into the souls of more than Crosby and, eventually, Hemingway himself. Hart Crane's book *The Bridge* appeared a few weeks after Crosby died. Three years later, Crane disappeared off the stern of a steamship while returning from Mexico to New York.

✻   ✻   ✻

At Le Dôme, Sinclair Lewis, flush with success after the publication of *Main Street* and enjoying a buzz brought on by a number of drinks, compared his writing to Flaubert's. He was cut short by a café patron who shouted, "Sit down. You're just a best-seller!" Lewis was not very popular with the Montparnasse

Above: Le Dôme in the late 1900s. (WSC)
Opposite: Le Dôme, on Boulevard Montparnasse, in the early 1900s. "In those days," Hemingway noted in A Moveable Feast, *"many people went to cafes at the corner of the Boulevard Montparnasse and the Boulevard Raspail to be seen publicly and in a way such places anticipated the columnists as the daily substitutes for immortality." (RV)*

crowd, which he referred to as a bunch of useless drunks. (Years later, Lewis himself struggled with alcoholism.) In an article he took his irritation out on Harold Stearns, whom he called "the very father and seer of the Dôme" and "an authority on living without laboring." Stearns responded, "The chief good point [of Montparnasse], of course, is that remotely, somehow, somewhere, even the dumbest American expatriates have been touched by the spiritual forces of French life." Like Hemingway, Lewis won a Nobel prize,

The restaurant La Mère Catherine has been on Place du Tertre in Montmartre for more than two hundred years. (WSC)

Mistinguett was once mentor to and lover of the debonair entertainer Maurice Chevalier. (WSC)

"He looks like a caricature of an American who has been run one half way through a meat chopper and then boiled, slightly, in oil."

It was typical behavior, for Hemingway tried to distance himself from those who wrote in the old-fashioned style, particularly that influenced by Henry James. Ever since his early days as a writer, when he was called a protégé of American novelist Sherwood Anderson, Hemingway tried to separate himself from the pack. Even his *The Torrents of Spring*, published in 1926, is a burlesque of Anderson's novel *Dark Laughter*, and also parodies the writing of other Hemingway contemporaries.

*   *   *

becoming the first American to win the award. That was in 1930, when Lewis was forty-five. Years later, in Venice, Lewis told Mary Hemingway, whom Ernest married in 1946, that her husband acted like a snob and had never responded in kind for Lewis's generous praise of *For Whom the Bell Tolls*. Hemingway indulged in his snobbery by complaining to the headwaiter of the Gritti that Lewis was a "bastard with a complexion that resembled the mountains of the moon." And in his novel *Across the River and into the Trees*, Hemingway describes a character — a writer — with Lewis's unusual looks: "He had a strange face like an over-enlarged, disappointed weasel or ferret." Later in the book, Hemingway offers another description of the same character:

On the Right Bank of the Seine, Hemingway would drop in at Café de la Paix, a historical monument of the Belle Epoque founded at the same time as the Paris Opera, in 1872. When they first arrived in Paris, the newly married Hemingways had Christmas dinner there, and when the bill came they discovered they had miscalculated the fare. While a nervous Hadley waited, Ernest ran the several miles back to their apartment to fetch money. The café appears in Hemingway's *The Sun Also Rises* and in the short story "My Old

62

*Harry's New York Bar on the
Right Bank. A small shrine
over the mantelpiece (inset)
features photographs of the
Hemingways. (WSC)*

Man." Thomas Wolfe and Henry James also used Café de la Paix in novels — Wolfe in *Of Time and the River*, and James in *The American*.

The most famous literary bar on the Right Bank, besides the Ritz (now called the Hemingway Bar), is the New York Bar. Founded in 1911, it is the oldest cocktail bar in Paris. In 1923, when Harry McElhone took over the place, where the Bloody Mary, the Sidecar and half a dozen other drinks were said to have been invented, it was renamed Harry's New York Bar. Hemingway was an occasional customer there for almost forty years. Harry served as Hemingway's second during boxing matches, and his son Andy (who eventually became the proprietor of Harry's) often played with the author's son, Jack. Customers would complain about the piano music wafting up from downstairs, unaware that the source was none other than George Gershwin, who was struggling to compose *An American in Paris*.

Harry's was popular with the press, especially *International Herald Tribune* writers, whose Paris office is in the neighborhood. A sign still in Harry's window reads "Sank Roo Doe Noo," so language-challenged Americans don't struggle over the French pronunciation of the bar's address, 5 Rue Daunou. Today, Americans are likely to visit the bar only because they had to make travel arrangements at the nearby main American Express office or had to change airline tickets at the United Airlines counter around the corner. Harry's New York Bar still looks like an English pub in Ivy League style, with college banners, old boxing gloves and tennis rackets hanging from the dark wood-paneled walls over the long wooden bar. The booths are still as comfortable as when Hemingway sat in them, and the owners have installed a small shrine of photographs of the author and of his son Jack.

* * *

Harry's address is written phonetically for American visitors. (WSC)

65

No other city in the world is as famous as Paris for its restaurants. During the *ancien régime*, eating a fine meal outside of the house was unheard of among French aristocrats until the first "luxury" restaurants opened, in the late 1700s. By the turn of the nineteenth century, Paris had 500 restaurants; by 1850, about 2,000.

After World War I, many people lived in small apartments with minimum cooking facilities, or in hotels with no cooking facilities at all. Restaurants were not a luxury but a necessity. They flourished, and by the time Hemingway arrived, in the 1920s, there were some 50,000 brasseries, bistros and restaurants — virtually one on every corner — whose clientele kept them busy almost twenty-four hours a day. By the 1930s there were so many eager patrons at the Hôtel Ritz restaurant that extra tables had to be set up in the hotel gallery.

Hemingway favored La Closerie des Lilas, La Coupole, Brasserié Lipp and, on the high end, the restaurants of the Hôtel Crillon and Hôtel Ritz, Maxim's and Fouquet's. He also sought out smaller finds. The conventional wisdom of the day was that one could find a bargain gourmet meal in Paris by looking for a restaurant with many crumbs on the tables, a fat madame and an old dog sleeping in the doorway.

As Hemingway described in *A Moveable Feast*, the American expatriate crowd also embraced French wine-drinking customs. "In Europe then we thought of wine as something as healthy and normal as food and also as a great giver of happiness and well being and delight," he wrote. "Drinking wine was not a snobbism nor a sign of sophistication nor a cult ..." Hemingway favored Cahors, a deep red wine of the Dordogne, and clarets. In his book *The Garden of Eden*, the main female character, Catherine, comments on Provence's Tavel rosé, another Hemingway favorite: "It is a great wine for people that are in love." Hemingway also wrote of wine in *The Sun Also Rises*, when Lady Brett holds up her glass and proposes a toast to royalty. Jake Barnes responded, "This wine is too good for toast-drinking, my dear. You don't want to mix emotions up with a wine like that. You lose the taste."

With restaurants, cafés and wine, Paris also offered a remarkable nightlife. In the 1920s, Le Moulin-Rouge got top billing for presenting Jazz Age singer Mistinguett (a lover and mentor of the young Maurice Chevalier),

long-forgotten. The brightest lights in the Parisian creative community were aware of the extraordinary confluence of talent around the River Seine. In her journal, Gertrude Stein wrote that "Pablo & [Henri] Matisse have a maleness that belongs to genius." She felt herself a full partner with them and the other avant-garde artists in their quest to invent new art.

Friendships were intense and intimate. Picasso, affecting American cowboy slang, called Stein "pard." But the motivations underlying their camaraderie were earnest: the Spaniard had Stein pose for him eighty times before deciding to wipe away the realistic portrait he had produced so that, using his "new" eyes, he could paint her not as she was in "reality" but as she appeared to him.

To Hemingway, Stein's jangling, lyrical repetitions, short sentences, disdain for adverbs and implicit emotions were as instructive as Picasso's abstractions of reality were inspirational to other painters. Hemingway once boasted to Sherwood Anderson that "Gertrude Stein and me are just like brothers" (an obvious reference to her lesbianism).

But the friendships of artistic Paris in the twenties also were fraught with jealousies and wounded pride. When, in Hemingway's opin-

A ballet costume design by the cubo-futurist Alexandra Exter, a Russian expatriate artist. Le Ballet Russe and Russian art were in vogue in Paris during the 1920s. (WSC)

ion, reviewers (and Stein herself) began to make too much of her influence on his writing, his loyalty to her diminished. Hemingway also later wrote that Stein "got to look like a Roman emperor and that was fine if you liked your women to look like Roman emperors." But more than anyone else, Stein encouraged Hemingway to give up newspaper work and to devote himself only to serious writing, come what may. Though their friendship waned, Stein opened Hemingway's eyes to modernism.

The alchemy of Paris, where older and younger artists became friends and shared their creative endeavors, worked its magic on

Hemingway and his colleagues. As Archibald MacLeish once put it, it was an atmosphere in which "working is not enough. There must be work accomplished, work beyond your farthest expectation of yourself."

*   *   *

Hemingway claimed the works of his favorite avant-garde painters — Cézanne in particular — depicted reality in ways that could be translated into a new kind of prose. He visited museums with that idea in mind — and, often, very little in his stomach. Hunger, he said, gave rise to a heightened ability to appreciate the artists' intent. Hemingway's appetite for art was not solely cerebral. Captivated by a Joan Miró oil called *The Farm*, Hemingway borrowed 5,000 francs from his friends to buy the painting, which he proudly brought home in a taxicab as a present for Hadley's thirty-fourth birthday. The Hemingways' new friend Gerald Murphy, one of the few American painters who invented *his* own style of painting (dubbed precisionism), assured Ernest that he had a fine eye and that the Miró was an excellent choice. Murphy was correct on both counts.

Gerald Murphy and his elegant wife Sara epitomized the artistically inclined Americans who made their way to Europe in the 1920s. Gerald, whose family owned the Mark Cross Company, had studied architecture at Yale before picking up the paintbrush. Stunned by the modernist paintings he had seen in Parisian galleries, he declared, "If that's painting, it's what I want to do."

Murphy's oversized paintings of ordinary objects, such as a watch or a safety razor, predated oversized pop-art images by forty years. A gifted dilettante merchant, Murphy was the inspiration for Dick Diver in Scott

Gerald and Sara Murphy's sign for their residence in the south of France, where Hemingway, Fitzgerald, Picasso and other luminaries of the literary and art worlds gathered. (EHMD)

Zelda and Scott Fitzgerald, photographed by Sara Murphy. (EHMD)

Fitzgerald's *Tender Is the Night*. Murphy and his wife were not only wealthy and prominent but also blessed with a social grace that transcended borders and language.

Murphy introduced Pablo Picasso to cubist painter Fernand Léger. Picasso was one of the only serious artists who actually liked Murphy's art, telling him that his paintings were simple, direct and distinctly American. Léger called Murphy "the only modern American painter today." American novelist John Dos Passos admired the "mathematical elegance" of Gerald's mind. Dos Passos also admitted that Murphy enabled him to visualize a "freshly invented world" in ordinary objects and, during their many walks, in the streets of Paris.

Murphy had studied painting with Natalia Goncharova, the Russian cubo-futurist painter who at the time was designing sets for ballet and theater. In the early twentieth century the Russian avant-garde was in vogue in Paris, and Goncharova hired Murphy to paint the backdrops for Sergey Diaghilev's dazzling Ballets

Cocktail, 1927, by Gerald Murphy. (EHMD)

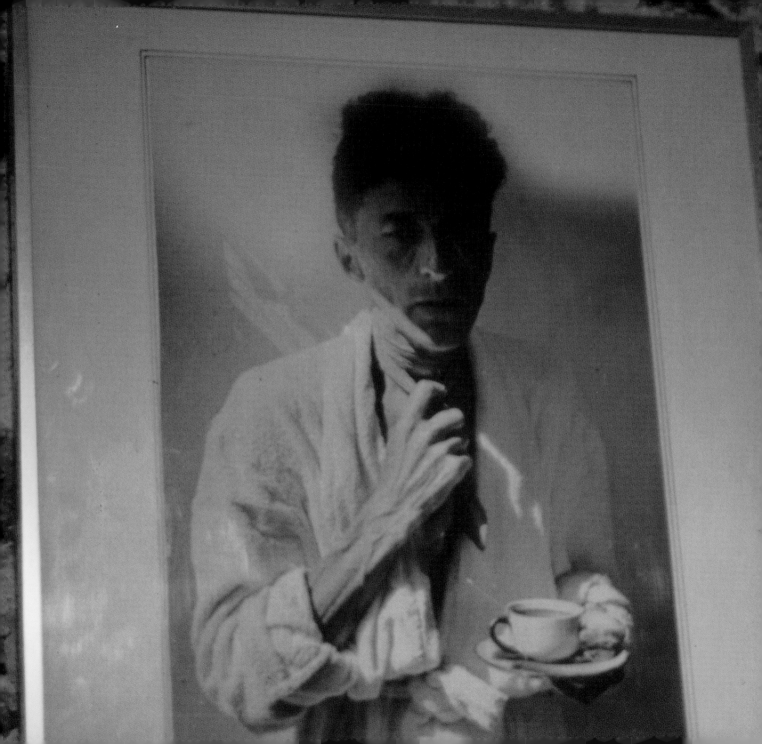

Right: Watch, *1925, by Gerald Murphy. (EHMD) Opposite: A photograph of artist Jean Cocteau, by Dada movement founder and surrealist Man Ray, hanging in the Jean Cocteau museum in Menton.*

Russes. Out of this and other projects Murphy fashioned distinctively American stage designs, the most typical of which includes the backdrop for Cole Porter's modernist ballet "Within the Quota". The piece features a gigantic newspaper whose front-page headline blares "Unknown Banker Buys the Atlantic," a spoof on the "yellow journalism" of William Randolph Hearst's newspaper empire, and on the machinations of American banking interests in Europe.

In the spring of 1927, the Murphys brought Hemingway to a preview perfor-

mance of Igor Stravinsky's opera *Oedipus Rex.* Along with them came the librettist, Jean Cocteau. Predictably, Hemingway found the whole affair arty and effete. At the time, Hemingway was vocally concerned about who was and who was not homosexual, and when Gerald generously loaned Hemingway his studio, he used Murphy's largesse to write a story entitled "A Simple Enquiry," about a homosexual officer who attempts to seduce an orderly.

Hemingway also befriended Jules Pascin, one of the finest café artists of the century.

Kiki of Montparnasse and the Japanese artist Foujita seated at the bar of Le Falstaff, which is still a popular watering hole in the 14th arrondissement. This ink-and-watercolor was produced by Oscar O'Fabre, a South American artist who painted in Paris in the 1920s and '30s. (WSC)

In a chapter in *A Moveable Feast*, Hemingway describes meeting the painter at Le Dôme after a good day's work. Notorious for sleeping with nearly all of his models, Pascin was accompanied by two of his latest muses. His dramatic suicide typified the improvisational extremes of the Parisian art world: after cutting his wrists, he wrote to his *régulière*, "*Adieu Lucy*," in blood on his studio door. Lying down to die, he immersed his wrists in the cold water of basins laid beside his mattress. But his blood coagulated, sealing his self-inflicted wounds. Determined to exit on schedule, he repaired to his kitchen, where he hanged himself from a cord. On the day of his funeral every art gallery in Paris closed its doors in tribute. So many mourners turned out that they blocked traffic for the five kilometers up to Saint-Ouen.

The social and even professional worlds of visual artists and writers overlapped in Hemingway's Paris. Hemingway and many of the city's finest artists — Picasso, Léger, surrealist Man Ray, Japanese artist Foujita — were friends who shared the sense that they were players in an extraordinary cultural phenomenon. It was in that spirit that Hemingway agreed in 1930 to write a preface for the memoirs of Kiki, a prominent Montparnasse artist's model (and lover of many of the artists for whom she posed). In his remarks Hemingway celebrated her as the female embodiment of the spirit of Paris in the twenties and as a gifted chronicler of her time. But Kiki's era was over, he concluded. Montparnasse had been transformed from a bohemian quarter to a "prosperous" district, "brightly lighted, dancinged, shredded-wheated." Even Kiki, he suggested, was, at age twenty-eight, nearing the end of her prime. Sara Murphy summed up the mood of the time with her famous observation, quoted in a profile by *The New Yorker* writer Calvin Tomkins, "It was like a great fair, and everybody was so young."

Hemingway sitting at Le Dôme, in an illustration by Jules
Pascin. (PC)

Chapter Five

Sports

"It was hard work but at Auteuil it was beautiful to watch each day they raced when you could be there and see the honest races with the great horses, and you got to know the course as well as any place you had ever known."

A MOVEABLE FEAST

Hemingway's passion for the sporting life was nearly boundless. His father, Dr. Clarence Edmonds Hemingway, nurtured young Ernest's love of the outdoors by taking him on hunting and fishing trips to Michigan's Lower Peninsula. Family summer sojourns to Walloon Lake, near the small town of Petoskey, provided background for many of

Opposite: Hemingway took pride in his boxing skills, as did sparring partners Jerry Manahan (left) and Jimmy Charters, an Englishman who ran the Dingo Bar and, later, Le Falstaff. (JFKL) Above: Charles Ritz, son of Cezar Ritz, founder of the famous hotel, avidly fished in Normandy as well as all over the rest of the world. (JFKL)

One of Hemingway's favorite tracks, Longchamps, on the outskirts of Paris. (WSC)
Opposite: The crowd at a skeet shooting contest that Hemingway attended in the 1930s in Monte Carlo. (JFKL)

the stories Hemingway struggled to write while in Paris — tales compiled for his first book, *In Our Time*, in 1925.

In France, Hemingway's enthusiasm for sports flourished. Both as spectator and participant, he studied the cultures of horse racing and bicycle racing, and pondered the arcane aspects of boxing and fishing. Though he wasn't a natural athlete, he had a competitive streak that influenced his approach to writing.

At times Hemingway felt jealous of his literary peers, most of whom he regarded as in-

ferior. They had invaded his territory by writing about subjects dear to him. Like a boxer, a bicyclist, or a jockey, Hemingway felt obliged to "train" harder. He rose early and wrote intensely, regarding his daily word count as a barometer of his dedication. He was determined to gain a competitive edge with wholly original material.

When Hemingway was not squinting down at a notebook, he and Hadley were likely to be in the stands at a thoroughbred horse-racing track. Racing — they later admitted to themselves that it was really "gambling" — played an important part in Hemingway's life in Paris. He would go out to Auteuil or Longchamps, on the outskirts of Paris, determined to learn everything he could, to get the "true gen" on the sport. For a time he considered himself a professional gambler. He got to know the jockeys, watched the horses in training, and talked to canny observers in the Parisian horse racing circuit, most notably Harold Stearns, who wrote a racing column under the pen name Peter Pickem for the Paris edition of *The Chicago Tribune*. Sometimes Stearns picked winners and sometimes he didn't, but he taught Hemingway the extremely useful racetrack skill of betting to

place. Stearns' savvy derived in part from his habits as a Montparnasse boulevardier. He kept a cell-like room on the rue Delambre, not far from the Dingo Bar, and patronized Le Sélect and Le Dôme, where he sponged drinks from friends and gathered tips on the races. Hemingway routinely consulted with Stearns, whose flashes of brilliance could yield a substantial return from a winning bet placed on a long shot.

A writer himself, Stearns also contrived to sell Hemingway's first book of short stories, *In Our Time*, to his New York publisher, Horace Liveright. Like Hemingway, Stearns had sailed, in 1921, from New York to escape what he and most American expatriates of that age regarded as the social mediocrity and oppression of Prohibition-era America. With thirty other intellectuals, he had written a diatribe titled *Civilization in the United States*, proclaiming America a cultural wasteland repressive to artists. Hoping to sort out his problems in the Parisian paradise, Stearns instead fell further into an abyss of vices. (Hemingway and Fitzgerald helped him by giving him money; Fitzgerald also arranged for one of Stearns's articles, "Apologia of an Expatriate," to be published in *Scribner's Maga-*

zine.) Stearns claimed to agree with Oscar Wilde's philosophy concerning temptations — that the "only truly absurd thing [was] not to yield to them." Stearns's undisciplined, erratic lifestyle made him an archetype of the lost generation, and Hemingway immortalized him as the alcoholic character Harvey Stone in *The Sun Also Rises*.

Still, there was more affection than vitriol in the free-floating camaraderie of Hemingway's Paris, even for the lost generation's most dissolute members. Hemingway's friend Evan Shipman — an American who later tutored Hemingway's son Jack in math using horse racing forms and odds figures — solicited help for Stearns from the American Aid Society, set up to assist destitute Americans in Paris. Sent back to America in 1932, Stearns was rescued from himself. With no teeth (they were removed at the American hospital in Neuilly because of an infection that was causing blindness), no luggage, and not a centime in his pocket, Stearns limped home. He soon headed out to the horse races, where his reputation as an expert preceded him, only to discover that, for him, the sport had lost its luster. He gave up horse racing, remarried, and embraced the pleasures of a quiet domestic life, hallmark of the world he had once scorned. His renewed enthusiasm for his homeland was such that he wrote several books in appreciation of America. It was a far cry from his bohemian rants at Le Dôme.

Hemingway fared better in Stearns's *Confessions of a Harvard Man* than Stearns did in *The Sun Also Rises*. When he was down on his luck in Paris, he wrote, Hemingway "did what he could — that is, he got my typewriter out of pawn, gave me cash, paid for my hotel, and tried to suggest one or two possible markets for my articles ... this much I can say for Hemingway — and I am glad to say, too: He always has acted the way you would expect a friend to act in all the years I have known him; he has never 'let me down' and, what I think I like best of all, he has always been honest with me."

Hemingway's own retreat from horse racing followed his assessment that it was taking too much time and costing too much money. "When I stopped working on the races I was glad but it left an emptiness," he wrote. He replaced his gambling habit with an immersion in bicycle racing. In those days bicycle races were held indoors, on sharply raked ovals such as Paris's Vélodrome, near the

Eiffel Tower. Journalist Sisley Huddleston described the scene at the time: "There while the unfortunate cyclists turn like squirrels, a motley throng assembles. It is after midnight that the spectacle is most astonishing. There is the populace of Paris, witty but impertinent, shouting encouragement and insult. There are the elegant revelers of Paris, wrapped in fur and glittering with diamonds. The rich on-lookers offer prizes to the competitors, and when they are not generous enough the 'populaires' hurl violent apostrophes at them, treating the women as 'poules de luxe.' The contrast between the rich idlers in their log-gias, with their champagne before them, and the masses in the galleries is amazing. A crude white light falls on this strange scene. The 'squirrels' turn, turn ..."

Ernest and Hadley sometimes brought a picnic basket to the race, and Ernest became so enamored with the sport he bought a bi-cycle. For a time he pedaled along the boule-vards of Paris in a racer's crouch, dressed as a cyclist in the Tour de France.

Novelist John Dos Passos joined Hemingway at many sporting events, including those at the Vélodrome. "I did enjoy going to the six day bi-cycle races with [Hemingway]," he wrote after

one of their visits. "The Six Jours at the Velo d' Hiver was fun. French sporting events had for me a special comical air that I enjoyed. We would collect, at the stalls and barrows of one of the narrow market streets we both loved, a quantity of wine and cheeses and crunch rolls, a pot of paté and perhaps a cold chicken, and sit up in the gallery. Hem knew all the statistics and the names and lives of the riders. His enthusiasm was catching but he tended to make a business of it while I just liked to eat and drink and to enjoy the show."

Hemingway was likely to be found ringside at the Cirque d' Hiver, studying the fighting styles of the professional boxers who fought there. He got to know the fighters and, on occasion, sparred with them. He was slow in the manner of most heavyweights. His vision was defective and his footwork could be clumsy, but as everyone who had gotten into the ring with him knew, his punches were as powerful as the kick of a mule. When he sparred with the pros, they acknowledged his value by paying him ten francs per match.

Hemingway often shared his enthusiasm for sports with friends who would seem unlikely to enjoy such events. After he took Sylvia Beach and Adrienne Monnier to a box-ing match, Beach wrote, "We were afraid they were going to bleed to death." However, she did have a good time, and Hemingway could be marvelous company, especially when involved with something about which he was passionate.

Whether he was throwing punches or casting a fishing line into the Seine, Hemingway strove to perform to his personal standards of excellence. And while in Paris he imposed the same standards on his literary pursuits. In his Nobel prize acceptance speech, in 1954, he took the notion further, expressing his conviction that self-realization requires us to venture beyond our imagined limits. To break new ground in literature, said Hemingway, a writer must go "far out past where he can go, out to where no one can help him."

Of the sports that most enthralled him — fishing, boxing, bullfighting, and big-game hunting — all were ultimately solitary activities. In the end, success in each depended not on a team effort but on the skills and focus of one person. In France, Hemingway sharpened his literary skills by focusing on the sports he loved.

Best wishes to Ernest Hemingway from Jimmy

When not sparring with Hemingway, Jimmy Charters, the former boxer from Liverpool and Dingo Bar manager, supplied his customers with tall tales and sports gossip. (JFKL) Inset: A hunter since boyhood, Hemingway enjoyed pheasant hunting in the Sologne region of France. (WSC)

93

Chapter Six

The South of France

Upon his arrival in Menton, following a 1927 motor trip through Fascist Italy, Hemingway declared the French Mediterranean town "very cheerful and clean and sane and lovely."

"CHE TI DICE LA PATRIA?" FROM *THE COMPLETE SHORT STORIES OF ERNEST HEMINGWAY*

That pronouncement fairly well summed up the feeling Hemingway had developed for the south of France. He was particularly taken with Provence, the southeastern region of the country, and he explored this area many times throughout his life, for it offered both natural beauty and sources of social and intellectual stimulation. "If Paris is a moveable feast,"

Opposite: Rudolph Valentino, 1920s silver-screen sex symbol, sunbathing on the beach in Antibes, a Côte d'Azur port and city in southeast France. Photo by Sara Murphy. (EHMD)
Above: Ernest Hemingway with son Bumby on the beach in Antibes. (EHMD)

Gerald Murphy's design for the ensign flag for his yacht, Weatherbird. *Picasso admired the flag, which seemed to wink in the Mediterranean breeze. (EHMD)*

most single-handedly transformed the south of France into a summer mecca for the well-heeled. People would say later that the couple practically invented the Côte d'Azur.

Gerald painted in a studio surrounded by orange trees, Mediterranean palms, and a vegetable garden. The Precisionist and the witty composer Cole Porter raked seaweed from La Garoupe beach, where soon bright lights such as Scott Fitzgerald, John Dos Passos, Archibald MacLeish, Dorothy Parker, Robert Benchley, Pablo Picasso, Jean Cocteau, Fernand Léger, and Igor Stravinsky would idle in the shade of the Murphys' beach umbrellas.

The Murphys were thoroughgoing aesthetes and innovators in nearly every endeavor they undertook, from "flower gala dinners" to daily group swims on the beach to cocktails prepared just so (and no more than two) on the verandah to the remodeling of their villa and the building their sailing ship *Weatherbird*, which had a recording of the song of the same name, played by Louis Armstrong, sealed in the keel. They lived their lives as a kind of performance art, with a seemingly effortless ease so entrancing to Scott Fitzgerald that he drew upon them to create Dick and Nicole Diver, husband and wife in his novel *Tender Is*

Hemingway's Provence author H.R. Stoneback observed, "then Provence is an infinite, glorious fête."

The lost generation's connection to southern France began in 1922 with Gerald and Sara Murphy's discovery of the city and port of Antibes, which up to then was favored only by the French as a winter vacation spot. Captivated by Antibes's Mediterranean vistas, the Murphys acquired a sprawling white house with a verandah overlooking the sea. They christened the house Villa América, and al-

Right: Among the picnickers at La Garoupe beach, 1923: Pablo Picasso (far left), Olga Picasso (center, in white), and Sara Murphy (lower right), wearing her ever-present string of pearls. Sara became Picasso's muse, inspiring more than two hundred studies, including "Woman in White," now at the Metropolitan Museum in New York. (EHMD)
Opposite: Sara Murphy (center), Phil Barry (partially hidden), and Gerald Murphy hanging upside down from the halyards of Weatherbird. *(EHMD)*

the Night: "The two Divers," he wrote, "began suddenly to warm and glow ... they seemed to speak to every one at the table singly and together, assuring them of their friendliness, their affection. And for a moment the faces turned up toward them were like the faces of poor children at a Christmas tree."

Besides the Fitzgeralds and Hemingways, the Antibe crowd included the silent-film sex symbol Rudolph Valentino, the cabaret singer Mistinguett, and the poet Archibald MacLeish. Anita Loos, the small-town California girl turned Hollywood screenwriter — now internationally acclaimed as the author of the comic novel *Gentlemen Prefer Blondes* — kept everyone amused with her razor-sharp wit. Picasso was joined by his wife Olga, a former Diaghilev ballet dancer, and his son Paulo.

It was generally acknowledged that all of the men were infatuated with Sara Murphy, to whom elegance came as naturally as breathing. She was never without a string of pearls loosely draped around her neck: Picasso drew a wonderful portrait of Sara, reclining on the

Right: Hemingway loved the Mediterranean and meditated on its charms in a passage in The Garden of Eden: *"He stood up and looked up and down the beach, corked the bottle of oil and put it in a side pocket of the rucksack and then walked down to the sea feeling the sand grow cool under his feet . . . Then he walked out and dove flat into the clear cold water and turned on his back and swam backstroke out to sea watching the beach beyond the steady beat of his legs and feet."* (WSC) *Below:* Picasso and his wife Olga, a former ballet dancer, on La Garoupe beach. The moment was captured by Sara Murphy's Kodak camera. (EHMD)

beach, wearing them and nothing else. "Sara est très festin," Picasso passionately repeated. Rumors flew, but that was as close as the famously promiscuous Spaniard ever got to Sara, as she was absolutely devoted to her tall and debonair husband.

*   *   *

In May 1926, while Ernest was in Spain, Hadley accepted the Murphys' invitation to move into the Villa América's guest house, hoping the sunshine would be good for Bumby's mysteriously persistent cough. Sara's doctor immediately diagnosed the boy's affliction as whooping cough, and mother and son were quarantined in the nearby Villa Paquita, which the Fitzgeralds were vacating for a larger place.

Upon Hemingway's arrival, the Murphys threw a champagne-and-caviar party at the little casino in Juan-les-Pins. Hadley saw that the Murphys, like so many others, had fallen for her husband, whom she described as irresistible, "the kind of man to whom men, women, children, and dogs were attracted."

Gerald Murphy, who made friends subtly, through charm, was in most ways the oppo-

Hadley Hemingway and son Bumby shortly after they arrived in Antibes. (EHMD)

site of Hemingway, who most often won people over by simply taking charge. But Murphy's assessment of Hemingway's commanding presence is among the most insightful to be found: "He was such an enveloping personality, so physically huge and forceful, and he overstated everything and talked so rapidly and so graphically and so well that you just found yourself agreeing with him."

Not all Villa América visitors saw it that way, however. Scott Fitzgerald felt his self-confidence ebb when Hemingway dominated

At one time or another, luminaries such as the Murphys, the Picassos, the Fitzgeralds and the Porters stayed at the Hôtel du Cap (now painted white) in Cap d'Antibes. Scott Fitzgerald described it in Tender Is the Night: "On the pleasant shore of the French Riviera, about half way between Marseilles and the Italian border, stands a large, proud, rose-colored hotel. Deferential palms cool its flushed facade, and before it stretches a short, dazzling beach."

Hemingway, Bumby (left front) and friends on the beach at Antibes. (JFKL)

a social setting. He rankled at the attention focused on his former protégé and lapsed into an unseemly display of childish jealousy that was compounded by intoxication. Among other antics, he draped a rug over his head during one gathering, crawled on the floor and wailed, "Sara is being mean to me!" Scott's wife Zelda, meanwhile, turned to Hemingway and confided that she thought that entertainer Al Jolson was greater than Jesus Christ. (Hemingway later confided to others that this was proof to him that Zelda was insane.)

The Murphys' young daughter, Honoria, later recalled that Hemingway taught the children how to clean fish in such a thoughtful and amusing way that none of them was repulsed by the blood and the offal. But the children's perceptions were not all focused on play. They sensed, said Honoria, that Scott Fitzgerald drank too much and that Zelda was a bit loony. As Linda Patterson Miller wrote in *Letters From the Lost Generation*, after publication of *Tender Is the Night*, in 1934, "most literary scholars came to agree with Ernest Hemingway's assessment that Dick and Nicole Diver represent a composite characterization of both the Murphys and the Fitzgeralds, and more the latter than the

former." Fitzgerald had merged Sara's image with Zelda's to make Nicole Diver a "psychopathic case," Hemingway said, and he had changed Gerald into "a self-portrait of Scott." As Hemingway saw it, Fitzgerald had captured the Murphys' "surface charm without comprehending their psychological complexities." Fitzgerald knew nothing of the Murphys' faults because he had "romanticized them."

It was the beginning of a dangerous summer. The Murphys temporarily banished Fitzgerald from their Antibes home follow-

Gerald Murphy dispensing mid-morning sherry on La Garoupe beach. At left is Dorothy Parker. (EHMD)

ing a dinner soirée during which the writer, very drunk, plucked a fig from a sorbet and threw it into the cleavage of one Princesse de Caraman-Chimay. Before long Zelda had cracked up, and Ernest and Hadley separated over Ernest's affair with Pauline Pfeiffer, a fashionable Paris-based writer for *Vogue* who was determined to make Ernest her husband.

Pfeiffer had commenced her campaign in Austria the previous winter, first becoming friends with Hadley and then increasingly inserting herself into the Hemingways' lives.

Now, in summer at the Villa América, there were three bicycles and three towels and three bathing suits hanging out to dry — always three of everything, and an unacknowledged sexual tension in the air. It was a painful time for Hadley, which Ernest would many years later render into fiction in his (posthumously published) novel *The Garden of Eden*.

Hemingway had his hands full dealing with the problems of being in love with both Hadley and Pauline, while Sara, always attracted to virile men, lavished attention on the upcoming

NORTHERN of FRANCE RY·WAGONS LITS Cᵒ·P.L.M.RYS

A NEW BLUE TRAIN TO THE COTE D'AZUR

Left: The quickest way from Paris to the Riviera was by train. (PC)
Below: Gerald and Sara Murphy on the beach at La Garoupe. (EHMD)

Right: Zelda, Frances ("Scottie") and F. Scott Fitzgerald rented a villa next to the Murphys' on Cap d'Antibes. (PUL)

Below: A fishing boat moored near Nice. In The Garden of Eden, Hemingway gives character David Bourne a moment of solitude to fish the Mediterranean: "He fished for some time with no luck and watched the mackerel boats tacking back and forth out on the blue sea and the shadows the high clouds made on the water. Then his float went under in a sharp descent with the line angling stiffly and he brought the pole up against the pull of a fish that was strong and driving wildly and making the line hiss through the water." (WSC)

writer. Her doting hurt Fitzgerald's feelings, for he was secretly in love with her and was in the process of rendering her into the fictional Nicole Diver. Zelda, however, was skeptical of Hemingway's machismo and said so, asserting that "nobody is as male as all that." Meanwhile, she was carelessly carrying on with a young French pilot from a nearby air base. "Everybody knew it but Scott," observed Sara sadly.

After Ernest and Hadley split up, the ever-generous Gerald Murphy offered the distraught writer his painting studio in Paris on the Rue Froidevaux. Below a thirty-foot-high ceiling, surrounded by Murphy's large canvases, Hemingway tried to concentrate on his writing while he and Hadley dismantled their domestic life.

In spite of the difficulties and heartbreak, it was a productive season for Hemingway. He showed the finished typescript of *The Sun Also Rises* to a sober Fitzgerald, who mixed praise with criticism, including the suggestion that Hemingway cut the first fifteen pages of unnecessary biographical information about the main characters. Hemingway took his advice.

*   *   *

Alert to violations against nature, Hemingway once remarked that the Côte d'Azur was being ruined by overdevelopment. But he could not wait to return. Subsequent trips took him to the real Provence — the Camargue — an island in the delta of the Rhône full of black bulls, white horses, and pink flamingoes. Hemingway had had enough of the Murphys' high-society celebrations, in which Yale buddies like Monty Woolley and Cole Porter, looking like penguins in black tie, rode tandem on Gerald's *motocyclette* through the narrow streets of Antibes.

Hemingway yearned for simpler pleasures and on their honeymoon he and Pauline bicycled along the Petit Rhône near Aigues-Mortes. "We are just gypsies. I am mad to *rouler*," Pauline wrote in 1927. The couple encountered real gypsies at Les Saintes-Maries-de-la-Mer, where Ernest and Pauline witnessed a religious celebration honoring an ancestor whom the gypsies, or *romanies*, consider a saint. Ernest had recently converted to Catholicism in order to marry Pauline, and was fascinated by its saints. In Les Saintes-Maries-de-la-Mer the celebration features a reenactment of the pilgrimage of Marie Salome and Marie Jacob, said to be

Every spring residents of Saintes-Maries-de-la-Mer carry these statues of Marie Salome and Marie Jacob from the local church to the seashore, in honor of their pilgrimage from ancient Palestine to the Mediterranean. (WSC)

close relatives of the Virgin Mary who are washed ashore in a small boat after being expelled from Judaea during the persecution. Marie Sara, a dark gypsy, brings the women to a spring where the village church now stands. There, she is baptized and goes on to convert other gypsies to Christianity.

The Vatican has yet to canonize Marie Sara, but to the gypsies *Sainte Sara* is their patron saint. Nowadays the celebration begins on May 24, when gypsies from all over Europe join Provençal people, clergymen, and *gardians* (cowboys on white horses) for a pilgrimage during which they carry statues of the Saints from the town church down to the sea. Ernest and Pauline participated in this commemoration, which in 1927 attracted about 2,000 of the pious. Today, the beach where the saints were said to have landed is crowded with some 40,000 celebrants, who gather for the observance.

The south of France drew Hemingway back many times more during his life, to better-known destinations such as Nice, Cannes, Avignon, and also to obscure places such as St. Gilles, Tarascon, Beaucaire, Pont du Gard, and Sète. He was fascinated by the world of the troubadours and knights of the Crusades and made research notes at the tower of Aigues-Mortes for a never-realized tale based on the Crusades.

During visits in 1949, in the fifties, and in 1960 — the twilight months of his darkening life — Hemingway still professed a profound love for his "very pleasant land of France." Here, in the summer of 1959, he enjoyed one of the happiest times of his life with wealthy friend Nathan "Bill" Davis, his fourth wife Mary Welsh, and his nineteen-year-old Irish secretary, Valerie Danby-Smith,

CARLTON HOTEL

Left: Once home to the Jazz Age crowd, the Carlton Hotel in Cannes is nowadays better known as a celebrity hangout during the city's annual film festival. (WSC)
Below: Sara Murphy. (EHMD)

Right: Hemingway loved to explore the back roads of France, where one often finds building advertisements like this one along the Route de Napoléon in Les Alpilles Maritimes. (WSC)
Below: The door handle of the church at St. Gilles, where Hemingway once stopped to admire the nearby abbey. (WSC)

who later joined the Hemingway clan by marrying Gregory Hemingway, son of Ernest and his second wife, Pauline Pfeiffer.

En route from Aigues-Mortes to Nîmes, the party stopped at Arles to pay homage to one of Hemingway's favorite painters, Vincent van Gogh, who came to Provence for the clarity of light and color. Hemingway was an ardent observer of artists' techniques and, after some quiet time spent before the vistas which once were the inspiration for van Gogh's colorful *impasto* style paintings, Hemingway confided to Valerie that he would have liked to write as well as van Gogh or Cézanne had painted.

"It was a thrill," Valerie later reflected, "to drive through that countryside in the waning of the summer, sharing his enthusiasm and delight as he compared the reality to canvas, life to art." She also noted that Hemingway "tended to exaggerate greatly, and mostly this was fun and enhanced every activity ... He had the most inquiring mind of anyone I've ever met. Although his knowledge was vast and diverse, he constantly deferred to those around him. Although he had been to Provence many times, on each visit it was as though he were seeing it for the first time."

Like van Gogh and Cézanne, Hemingway came of age as an artist in the city, yet went on to find some of his richest material in the natural world. It was in the south of France that he gathered many of the most delicious vignettes for *A Moveable Feast*. It also was where he found the sultry, sun-bleached setting for his boldly experimental novel *The Garden of Eden*, an exploration of androgyny that, when published posthumously, in 1986, refuted critics who had accused Hemingway of hidebound literary machismo.

Scott, Scottie and Zelda Fitzgerald in the Mediterranean near Antibes. (EHMD)

Chapter Seven

World War II

"Know what you fight for and where and why and to what ends."

LETTER TO MARY WELSH, 1944, FROM ERNEST HEMINGWAY

Even as more and more of his readers came to regard him as the archetypal member of the Paris-based expatriate American literary world immortalized in *The Sun Also Rises*, Hemingway longed to return home. He moved to Key West — a long way and a far cry from France, where henceforth he would visit but never again reside. Throughout the remainder of his life,

Opposite: Hemingway on his motorcycle in Normandy, July 1944. Above: Hemingway used binoculars to report on the war, but also took up arms to fight in it. (JFKL)

Hemingway (left) quickly made friends with Colonel Charles "Buck" Lanham (center). (JFKL)

however, whether writing in the carriage house behind his Key West home, or in Idaho or Cuba, he would return to the cradle of his creative career for settings for his fictional tales.

The popular take on Hemingway in the second half of the 1930s is of his participation in the Spanish Civil War, and the subsequent publication of his great novel *For Whom the Bell Tolls*. (As a journalist, Hemingway proved prescient when he called Spain's thirty-two-month rebellion a dress rehearsal for a full-blown European war, which he predicted would break out before the end of 1939.) Hemingway's forays to Iberia, however, always took him through France, which remained his primary European headquarters. He managed to spend many weeks in Paris, squiring young writer Martha Gellhorn and introducing her to many of his lost-generation cohorts. Less publicized were quiet getaway auto tours with Gellhorn, his soon-to-be third wife, through the French countryside, and a pheasant hunting sojourn in the Sologne region.

Hemingway and Martha resided in his tropical Cuban hideaway during the first half of World War II, but he missed France, now off-limits because of the German occupation. In December of 1940 he lamented in a letter to Sara Murphy that "the only things I care about really like caviar and France and Africa you can't go to anymore."

Yearning to be at the front, Martha left for Europe to cover the war. Ernest, increasingly exasperated by Martha's unwillingness to abandon her journalistic career and play a wifely role, threatened to follow her to the continent, "kick her ass good" and order her home — or to military school.

When Hemingway entered Paris during the Liberation, sections of the city were still under fire. (JFKL)

churches in France. He prayed at the Chapel of our Lady of the Pillar, *La Chapelle du Pilier*. It was a kind of spiritual homecoming, for it was in Chartres, in 1925, that he had seized this passage from the Book of Ecclesiastes for the title for his first major novel: "One generation passeth away, and another generation cometh; but the earth abideth forever ... The sun also ariseth, and the sun goeth down, and hasteth to the place where he arose ..."

The following year, Hemingway and poet Archibald MacLeish journeyed to Chartres by bicycle. Hemingway would return again throughout his life. His affection for the city and its great church inspired the nickname "Pilar," which he bestowed upon Pauline, his second wife, and, later, his fishing boat. His ritual during visits to the cathedral never varied: he lit candles and offered prayers for the souls of those he cherished. On Wednesday, August 23, Général Charles de Gaulle visited that same church, where huge crowds shouted outside, "Vive de Gaulle!" He did not linger but pressed on to the old presidential palace in Rambouillet.

At the Château de Rambouillet Général Jacques Leclerc found the future president of France smoking English cigarettes and reading Molière's *Le Bourgeois Gentilhomme*. Leclerc told de Gaulle he was going to take Paris with the Allied troops. They both knew it had to be done swiftly, and de Gaulle gave his blessing: "Go fast! We cannot have another *Commune*."

That same evening, unaware of de Gaulle's secret meeting, Hemingway and Colonel Bruce were presented to a stern looking Leclerc. Always quick to take command, Hemingway immediately offered advice to the general on the best way to get to Paris, and he

125

American soldiers and tanks liberating Paris in August 1944. (JFKL)

King, and your armored correspondent withdrew." Hemingway later referred to the general as "that jerk Leclerc."

General Dwight Eisenhower, the Supreme Allied Commander, postponed taking Paris for as long as possible, hoping his armies could fight the Germans in open country, where his armor could maneuver more effectively. There was another consideration. The Allied forces consumed gasoline voraciously. Fuel shortages worried Eisenhower's logistical planners, for the Allies had to have sufficient reserves in order to breach the Germans' Siegfried Line and establish a bridgehead over the Rhine before winter snows commenced.

Saving the City of Light from destruction was imperative, but Eisenhower feared that a premature assault on an occupied Paris without first routing the German Army was certain to trigger a campaign of street battles. The city well might be ruined and suffer a counterattack. Eisenhower embarked on his strategy of engagement, but as August came to a sultry end, it seemed the best strategy was for the Allies to take Paris.

Adolf Hitler, who had twice before attacked the city, now found himself in the historically ironical position of having to

bragged about the intelligence he had acquired. But after four years of fighting the Italians and the Germans, Leclerc wasn't about to take advice from a war correspondent turned amateur soldier. He told Hemingway that he should go indulge in sexual intercourse on vacation. Hemingway described the scene more delicately in his October 1944 *Collier's* article "How We Came to Paris": "Buzz off, you unspeakable, the gallant Général said, in effect, in something above a whisper and Colonel B (Bruce), the résistance

TOROS
BAYONNE-BIARRITZ

DIMANCHE 16 AOUT 1959

Chapter Eight

Bullfights

"… the bullfight is very
moral to me because I feel
very fine while it is going
on and have a feeling
of life and death and
mortality and immortality,
and after it is over I feel
very sad but very fine."

DEATH IN THE AFTERNOON (1932)

More than any other writer, Hemingway is
responsible for bringing the arcane art of bullfighting to the attention of the English-
speaking world. He followed the bullfight
circuits during most of his adult life, and most
intensely during his Paris years in the 1920s
and the 1950s. Though his landmark treatise
on bullfighting, *Death in the Afternoon*, derived

*Opposite: French-style bullfights are not intended to end with the
death of the bull. Here a Camarguais bullfighter dashes away
after trying to snatch a ribbon from the bull's back. (WSC)
Above: Hemingway attended the 1959 Bayonne-Biarritz bullfight
advertised in this brochure. The event starred the matador Jaime
Ostos. (WSC)*

Picadors lance the bull's neck muscles to lower the animal's horns. (WSC)

mainly from his Spanish expeditions, his trips to the hinterlands of France contributed significantly to his knowledge of the ritual.

Hemingway attended events in Arles, Biarritz, and Nîmes, and in various small French hamlets. Through his writing he came to be regarded as a leading aficionado, a term Hemingway himself defined in *Death in the Afternoon*. "The aficionado, or lover of the bullfight," he wrote, "may be said, broadly, then, to be one who has this sense of the tragedy and ritual of the fight so that the minor aspects are not important except as they relate to the whole. Either you have this or you have not, just as, without implying any comparison, you have or have not an ear for music."

Men have confronted bulls in ritual combat in France since Roman times. The earliest Gallic bullfights took place in amphitheaters in one of Rome's far-flung provinces, the sun-drenched region of Provence. Unlike the Spanish fights, where the bull must die, in the Provençal spectacle the animals are spared. If, as Hemingway insisted, the Spanish bullfight is a form of tragedy, then the French bullfight is a kind of comedy. The human contestants enter the ring without cape or sword. Rather than advancing bravely to confront and dominate the bull with the elaborate and dangerous choreography for which Spanish bullrings are famous, French bullfighters are permitted to run from it. (In an Iberian *corrida*, such behavior would be tantamount to cowardice.)

In Spain bulls selected for the ring are never permitted to see a man on foot until they enter the arena (lest they prematurely determine how the two-legged creatures side-step their horns). In France fighting bulls arrive without that disadvantage. Thus the Provençal runners, whose goal is to snatch a colored ribbon from the back of the bull's neck, must work very close to the animal's horns. Death in the French bullring is rare, as the bull's horns are usually shaved down or

Above: A photomontage postcard featuring Cole "Anything Goes" Porter wearing the "suit of lights" typically seen on Spanish bullfighters. (EHMD)
Right: A French bullfighter in Arles barely escapes the bull's horns. (WSC)

Chapter Nine

The Feast Moves On

"When I dream of afterlife in heaven, the action always takes place in the Paris Ritz. It's a fine summer night. I knock back a couple of martinis in the bar, Cambon side. Then there's a wonderful dinner under a flowering chestnut tree in what's called 'le Petit Jardin.' That's the little garden that faces the Grill. After a few brandies I wander up to my room and slip into one of those huge Ritz beds. They are all made of brass. There's a bolster for my head the size of the Graf Zeppelin and four square pillows filled with real goose feathers — two for me, and two for my quite heavenly companion."

HEMINGWAY, IN A LETTER TO A FRIEND

Opposite: Hemingway and his touring car and driver. The author journeyed to the south of France and to Spain in the summer of 1959. (WSC) Above: Hemingway used the martini to toast the liberation of the Ritz Hotel during World War II, ordering seventy-three martinis for his irregular soldiers and his friends. (WSC)

After Hemingway's death, several books, some wildly inaccurate, were published to capitalize on the Hemingway myth. (WSC)

Hemingway traveled to Europe in 1954, 1956 and 1959, and made his last trip there in 1960. Each of these journeys included extended visits to France, a country he once called home. Although France is the setting for three of his books — *The Sun Also Rises, A Moveable Feast* and *The Garden of Eden* — it is referred to frequently in his other books by many of his characters: Thomas Hudson in *Islands in the Stream,* Harry in "The Snows of Kilimanjaro" and the narrator in *Green Hills of Africa.*

Hemingway developed a deep nostalgia for his first years in Paris, where he had found such profound inspiration for his work. Recalling sybaritic idylls in the 1920s with his first wife, Hadley Richardson, and later with Pauline Pfeiffer, Hemingway began to work on a remarkable novel. Appropriately titled *The Garden of Eden,* it is about a young American writer and his

wealthy spouse commencing their married life with an indolent sojourn in the south of France. The novel offers unique insights into the emotions that France inspired in Hemingway, and the little events and rituals that made up his days as an expatriate in that astonishingly creative era. Also, during these last extended stays in France Hemingway gathered material for *A Moveable Feast,* which would become one of the loveliest memoirs ever in literature.

At the end of the summer of 1959, which was full of parties and the hectic, nerve-wracking hegira of the bullfighting circuit, Hemingway ended up at the Hôtel Ritz in Paris, once again sick. This time it was just a bad cold, a fever and an infected kidney for which he was still gulping pills when he boarded the *Liberté* to sail home.

One of his fellow passengers turned out to be Andrew Turnbull, who had been in Paris gathering material for a biography on F. Scott Fitzgerald. Hemingway was not eager to share the secrets of *his* three chapters on Fitzgerald in *A Moveable Feast,* which were in his briefcase in his stateroom. At the Hôtel Ritz, Charles Ritz had found an old trunk of Hemingway's which contained his Paris notes, from which Hemingway would write so poetically about Scott Fitzgerald: "His talent was as natural as the pattern that was made by the dust on

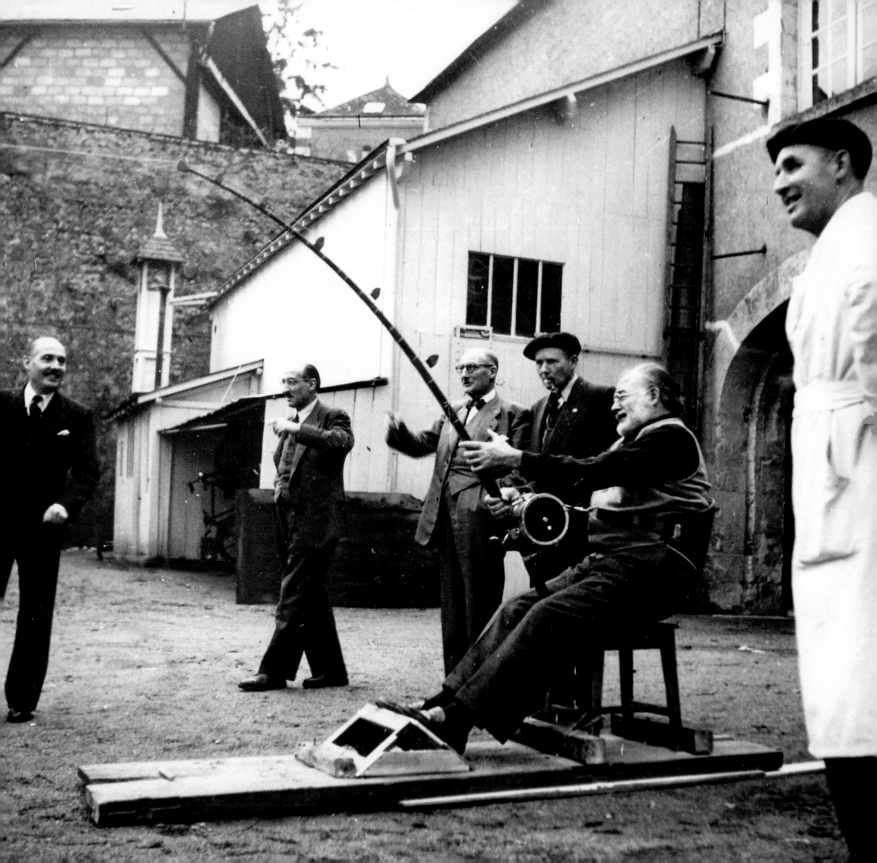

butterfly's wings. At one time he understood it no more than the butterfly did and he did not know when it was brushed or marred. Later he became conscious of his damaged wings and of their construction and he learned to think and could not fly any more because the love of flight was gone and he could only remember when it had been effortless."

Hemingway put off Turnbull until the last day at sea when he finally agreed to meet him at the bar. The biographer found a rather haggard Hemingway, his once powerful bare forearms meager and the whites of his eyes veined with red. Hemingway looked over Turnbull "with a kind of grazing diffidence." Although he found Hemingway "staged and put on," Turnbull added that "a great dignity flowed from his tall lurching frame and his sad mask of a face."

Some of Hemingway's insecurities surfaced in his later years during conversations with author Budd Shulberg, who worked with Fitzgerald on Hollywood screenplays and met Hemingway in Key West and Cuba. Shulberg recounted how Hemingway responded with malicious remarks to mention of Fitzgerald's kindness in referring him to his editors at Scribner's and helping him with money and professional guidance.

"What a jackass Papa was about fellow writers," Shulberg wrote in a 1999 letter to my father, Barnaby Conrad, whose 1952 book about bullfighting, *Matador*, was in competition with Hemingway's writings on the subject. "Always found it odd he could be so sensitive in some areas, and write so well, and so myopic and dog-in-the-manger in others . . . He could lap up praise all right. What bugged him was anyone entering into areas he felt were his by eminent domain, bullfighting for you, boxing for me, war for Irwin [Shaw]. I never forgave him, aside from my own slights for his ingratitude and boorishness to Scott, who went to bat for him early on in a way EH would never have reciprocated."

Hemingway in fact had begun having difficulty keeping the words flowing, which was most devastating to a man for whom writing was a religion. He was having an especially hard time with the ending of *A Moveable Feast*, which he rewrote dozens of times. The well of wine — of words — had finally run dry.

After being treated for acute depression and alcoholism at the Mayo Clinic in Minnesota, he set to work arranging the sequence for his Paris notebook. Shock treatments had handicapped his memory, the most valuable tool for writing, and sometimes it took him a week to write a satisfactory sentence. He missed his vast

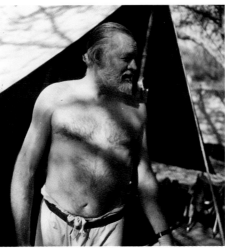

Left: Hemingway on safari in Africa, where he suffered severe injuries in two plane crashes. (JFKL)
Opposite: John Bryson shot this famous picture, less than a year before Hemingway's death, in Sun Valley, where Hemingway wrote A Moveable Feast. *He concluded the memoir with his observation that "There is never any ending to Paris and the memory of each person who has lived in it differs from that of any other . . . Paris was always worth it and you received return for whatever you brought to it. But this is how Paris was in the early days when we were very poor and very happy."*

library and asked Charles Scribner's Sons to send copies of *The Oxford Book of English Verse* and the King James version of the Bible where he hoped to find a title for his Paris memoirs.

Charles Scribner wrote to Hemingway and reminded him of his lifelong motto, *"Il faut (d'abord) durer."* To quote biographer Carlos Baker, that notion had been succeeded by another: " *'Il faut (après tout) mourir.'* The idea, if not the phrase, filled all his mind."

After years of suffering from physical pain from two African safari plane crashes, as well as emotional pain, Hemingway committed suicide at first light on July 2, 1961.

He left behind a remarkable amount of published material — countless magazine and newspaper articles, twenty-eight books and more than fifty short stories. His publications still earn substantial royalties.

If Hemingway could come back to life for a day, he might very well elect to spend it in France. On this day he would perhaps write a few words over a café crème in La Closerie des Lilas, stand outside and salute his old friend, the statue of the nineteeth-century French marshal, Michel Ney, and stroll through the Luxembourg Gardens. He would pass by the statue of Flaubert under chestnut trees in blossom, pass Place St-Sulpice and stroll down by St-Germain-des-Prés. He might sit at a table at Les Deux-Magots café and watch the Parisian life parade by. Then he would cross the street to the Brasserié Lipp for sausage and potatoes cooked in oil, washing it down with a cold *demi-pression*. There would be more walking, over one of the bridges of the River Seine, through the Tuileries Gardens to l'Orangerie and to museums to view his favorite Cézanne paintings before heading off to Longchamps or Auteuil to watch the horse races. A winner? It wouldn't matter. *Ambiance!*

LE SANS-...CI

IL 1860.

Prix : 10 centimes

LE MASQUE
SEMAINE THÉATRALE ILLUSTRÉE
PARAISSANT TOUS LES JEUDIS
N° 199. — Dix centimes.
(15 centimes dans les départements et dans les gares de chemin de fer.)

JOURNAL POUR TOUS
MAGASIN HEBDOMADAIRE ILLUST

Deuxième année. — Prix : C...

LA GAU...LE
Journal de Joyeux Récits, C...
PARAISSANT DE...

...froy-Marie

Jeudi 28 Juillet 1892.

ABONNEMENTS
PARIS ET PROVINCE
Un an....... 7 fr.
Six mois.... 4 »
Trois mois.. 2 »
Étranger, port en plus.

5, Rue Geoffroy-Marie
PARIS

...ivement pour...
...son boudoir, ...
...ique cela.
...u — Je l'explique pas...
...tu n'étais pas...
...tu as aimé c...
...re, peut-être...
...abandre se lev...
...les épaules de...
— Je vais te di...
...nière, au mo...

...l'ait détachée de moi. Grand Dieu !
...mande quel charme elle peut trouver
...sistence intolérable.
...se connais pas mieux les femmes ?
...rave cette volupté raffinée, exquise,
...rembler, ramper devant elle un homme
...nes six pouces, ayant bravé la mort
...— quoi dit sans le flatter,
...très beau...
...pourrait, toute superbe qu'elle est,
...terre d'une chiquenaude. Une seule
...onne...

20 CENTIMES

1er Février 1903

l'Amour
JOURNAL ILLUSTRÉ PARAISSANT LE MARDI
FRANCE UN AN 11 fr. SIX MOIS 6 fr.

Troisième Année. — N° 75.

EXIGER ...
30 Centimes le N...

Dimanche 15 Janvier 1882

Selected Bibliography

Allan, Tony. *The Glamour Years Paris 1919-40.* New York: Gallery Books, a division of W.H. Smith Publisher Inc./Bison Books Corp., 1977.

Anderson, Chester G. *James Joyce and His World.* New York: Charles Scribner's Sons, 1968.

Baker, Carlos. *Ernest Hemingway: A Life Story.* New York: Charles Scribner's Sons, 1969.

Beach, Sylvia. *Les Ecrivains Americains a Paris et Leur Amis 1920-1930.* New York: Le Centre Culturel Americain/Shakespeare and Company/Harcourt, Brace and Company, 1959.

Brian, Denis. *The True Gen: An Intimate Portrait of Ernest Hemingway by Those Who Knew Him.* New York: Grove Press, 1987.

Bruccoli, Matthew J. *Fitzgerald and Hemingway, A Dangerous Friendship.* New York: Caroll & Graf Publishers, Inc., 1994.

Bruccoli, Matthew J.; Smith, Scottie Fitzgerald; and Kerr, Joan P. *The Romantic Egoists, A Pictorial Autobiography from the Scrapbooks and Albums of Scott and Zelda Fitzgerald.* New York: Charles Scribner's Sons, 1974.

Burgess, Anthony. *Ernest Hemingway and His World.* New York/London: Thames and Hudson, 1978.

Charters, James, and Cody, Morrill. *This Must Be the Place: Memoirs of Jimmie the Barman.* New York: Lee Furman, Inc., 1937.

Collins, Larry, and Lapierre, Dominique. *Is Paris Burning?* New York: Simon and Schuster, 1965.

Conover, Anne. *Caresse Crosby.* Santa Barbara: Capra Press, 1989.

Conrad, Barnaby. *La Fiesta Brava, The Art of the Bull Ring.* Boston: Houghton Mifflin Company, 1950.

_____. *Hemingway's Spain.* San Francisco: Chronicle Books, 1989.

Cowley, Malcolm. *A Second Flowering, works and days of the lost generation.* New York: The Viking Press, 1973.

Cross, Robert. *Henry Miller: The Paris Years.* Big Sur: Peeramid, 1991.

Donnelly, Honoria Murphy, with Billings, Richard N. *Sara & Gerald: Villa America and After.* New York: Times Books, 1982.

Opposite: These old Parisian journals, hanging in a storefront window, predate Hemingway's literary-magazine years. (WSC)

Fitch, Noel Riley. *Sylvia Beach and the Lost Generation.* New York/London: W.W. Norton & Company, 1983.

_____. *Literary Cafes of Paris.* Washington/Philadelphia: Starrhill Press, 1989.

_____. *Walks In Hemingway's Paris.* New York: St. Martin's Press, 1989.

Flanner, Janet. *Paris Was Yesterday: 1925-1936.* San Diego/New York/London: Harcourt Brace Jovanovich Publishers, 1988.

Ford, Hugh. *Four Lives in Paris.* San Francisco: North Point Press, 1987.

Gajdusek, Robert E. *Hemingway's Paris.* New York: Charles Scribner's Sons, 1978.

_____. *Hemingway and Joyce: A Study in Debt and Payment.* Corte Madera: Square Circle Press, 1984.

Griffin, Peter. *Less Than a Treason: Hemingway in Paris.* New York/Oxford: University Press, 1990.

Haight, Mary Ellen Jordan. *Walks in Gertrude Stein's Paris.* Salt Lake City: Pereguine Smith Books, Gibbs M. Smith, Inc., 1988.

Hemingway, Ernest. *In Our Time.* New York: Charles Scribner's Sons, 1925.

_____. *The Sun Also Rises.* New York: Charles Scribner's Sons, 1926.

_____. *Death in the Afternoon.* New York: Charles Scribner's Sons, 1932.

_____. *A Moveable Feast.* New York: Charles Scribner's Sons, 1964.

_____. *By-Line: Ernest Hemingway, Selected Articles and Dispatches of Four Decades,* edited By William White. New York: Charles Scribner's Sons, 1967.

_____. *Ernest Hemingway Selected Letters: 1917-1961.* New York: Charles Scribner's Sons, 1981.

_____. *"The Dangerous Summer."* New York: Charles Scribner's Sons, 1985.

_____. *Dateline Toronto: The Complete Toronto Star Dispatches, 1920-1924,* edited by William White. New York: Charles Scribner's Sons, 1985.

_____. *The Garden of Eden.* New York: Charles Scribner's Sons, 1986.

_____. *The Complete Short Stories of Ernest Hemingway: The Finca Vigia Edition.* New York: Charles Scribner's Sons, 1987.

Hemingway, Gregory H. *Papa: A Personal Memoir.* New York: Paragon House Publishers, 1976.

Hemingway, Jack. *Misadventures of a Fly Fisherman: My Life With and Without Papa.* Dallas: Taylor Publishing Company, 1986.

Hemingway, Marcelline Sanford. *At the Hemingways.* Moscow, Idaho: University of Idaho Press, 1999.

Hemingway, Valerie. *The Garden of Eden Revisited: With Hemingway in Provence in the Summer of '59.* The Hemingway Review Centennial Issue. Moscow, Idaho: University of Idaho Press/The Ernest Hemingway Foundation, 1999.

Hotchener, A. E. *Papa Hemingway.* New York: Random House, 1966.

_____. *Hemingway And His World.* New York/Paris: The Vendome Press, 1989.

Johnson, Douglas and Madeleine. *The Age of Illusion: Art and Politics in France 1918-1940.* New York: Rizzoli, 1987.

Junkins, Donald. *Hemingway's First Corrida de Toros*. North Dakota Quarterly Vol. 64, no. 3. Grand Forks: University of North Dakota, 1997.

Kert, Bernice. *The Hemingway Women*. New York: W.W. Norton & Company, 1983.

Kiki. *The Education of a Model,* originally *Souvenirs Kiki* and *Kiki's Memoirs*, translated into English by Samuel Putnam, with an introduction by Ernest Hemingway. New York: Boars Head Books, 1950.

Kluver, Billy, and Martin, Julie. *Kiki's Paris: Artists and Lovers 1900-1930*. New York: Harry N. Abrams, Inc., 1989.

Knopf Guides. *Restaurants of Paris*. New York: Alfred A. Knopf Inc., 1944. Originally published in Paris by Nouveaux-Loisers, a subsidiary of Gallimard, 1993.

Lynn, Kenneth S. *Hemingway*. Cambridge, Mass./London: Harvard University Press, 1987.

McAlmon, Robert and Boyle, Kay. *Being Geniuses Together: 1920-1930*. San Francisco: North Point Press, 1984.

Mellow, James R. *Charmed Circle: Gertrude Stein & Company*. New York/Washington: Praeger Publishers, 1974.

_____. *Hemingway: A Life Without Consequence*. New York/London: Houghton Mifflin Company, 1992.

Miller, Linda Patterson. *Letters from the Lost Generation*. New Brunswick and London: Rutgers University Press, 1991.

Putnam, Samuel. *Paris Was Our Mistress, Memoirs of a Lost & Found Generation*. New York: The Viking Press, 1947.

Reynolds, Michael. *Hemingway: The Paris Years*. Oxford, England, and Cambridge, Mass.: Blackwell, 1989.

_____. *Hemingway: The American Homecoming*. Oxford, England, and Cambridge, Mass.: Blackwell, 1992.

_____. *Hemingway The 1930s*. New York/London: W.W. Norton & Company, 1997.

_____. *Hemingway: The Final Years*. New York/London: W.W. Norton & Company, 1999.

Schulberg, Budd. *Sparring With Hemingway and Other Legends of the Fight Game*. Chicago: Ivan R. Dee, 1995.

Stearns, Harold E. *The Confessions of a Harvard Man*. Santa Barbara: The Paget Press/Sutton West, 1984.

Stoneback, H.R. *Hemingway's Happiest Summer*. North Dakota Quarterly, vol. 64, no. 3. Grand Forks: University of North Dakota, 1997.

Tomkins, Calvin. *Living Well Is the Best Revenge*. New York: The Viking Press, 1971.

Vaill, Amanda. *Everybody Was So Young*. Boston/New York: Houghton Mifflin Company, 1998.

Whiting, Charles. *Papa Goes to War: Ernest Hemingway in Europe, 1944-45*. Marlborough: The Crowood Press, 1990.

Acknowledgments

I would like to thank Woodford Press publishers Daniel Ross and David Burgin, editors Richard Defendorf and Mark Miller, book designer Tom Morgan, Hemingway biographer Michael Reynolds, and Hemingway scholars H.R. Stoneback, Robert Gajdusek, Linda Patterson Miller and Matthew J. Bruccoli. Writers Amanda Vaille, Paco Taylor, Budd Shulberg, and my father, Barnaby Conrad, offered valuable insights for this project. I also want to thank Scribner's, a division of Simon & Schuster, for permission to publish excerpts from Hemingway's works. I am grateful to the Ernest Hemingway Society for presenting conferences on Hemingway's life and works, and to the Ernest Hemingway Foundation, which in 1999 played host to the Hemingway Centennial celebration in Oak Park, Illinois, where Patrick Hemingway spoke about editing his father's posthumous novel *True at First Light*. My thanks to Jack Hemingway for the invitation to his seventy-fifth birthday celebraion in Ketcham, Idaho, and to Mariel Hemingway for her informative documentary on her grandfather. John Sanford (whose mother was Marcelline Hemingway, Ernest's sister) offered insights into the family legacy, and Valerie Hemingway generously described her travels with the author in the south of France. Thanks also to John Donnelly and the estate of Honoria Murphy Donnelly for the use of some wonderful illustrations, and to the photo archivists at Princeton University Library and the John F. Kennedy Library of Boston. Also most helpful were my sons Anthony and Will James, who assisted with camera equipment during our journeys through France. Finally, my thanks to Maurice Neville, Gregory Hemingway, Barnaby Conrad III, and Daisy Donovan.

Index

A check from Ernest Hemingway to Caresse Crosby, owner of Black Sun Press and Crosby Continental Editions, which published some of Hemingway's early writing, including a European edition of The Torrents of Spring. Caresse was very generous, and this check was likely a repayment of a loan.

PHOTO-CREDIT KEY
(BMA) Baltimore Museum of Art
(DMA) Dallas Museum of Art
(EHMD) Estate of Honoria Murphy Donnelly
(JFKL) John F. Kennedy Library
(PUL) Princeton University Library
(PC) Private Collection
(RV) Roger Violet
(WSC) Winston Stuart Conrad

VRIL 1860.

Prix : 40 centimes

LE MASQUE

SEMAINE THÉATRALE ILLUSTRÉE

PARAISSANT TOUS LES JEUDIS

N° 199. — Dix centimes.

(15 centimes dans les départements et dans les gares de chemins de fer.)

JOURNAL POUR TOU

MAGASIN HEBDOMADAIRE ILLUST